BIBLE STUDY
Workbook for Kids

Lessons, Activities, Quizzes, and Questions to Deepen Your Faith

JENNY INGRAM

callisto publishing
an imprint of Sourcebooks

Dear parents, Jesus tells us,
"Go and make disciples." I pray this book inspires
your child's curiosity about God and heartens your
discipleship journey with your children.

Copyright © 2024 by Callisto Publishing LLC
Cover and internal design © 2024 by Callisto Publishing LLC
Illustrations © Patrick Corrigan with the following exceptions: © miniwide/Shutterstock (bible); © Sarah Rebar (heart); © Robin Boyer (leaf); © VolodymyrSanych/Shutterstock (cover texture)
Art Director: Michael Cook
Art Producer: Sue Bischofberger
Editor: Laura Apperson
Production Editor: Holland Baker
Production Manager: David Zapanta

Callisto Publishing and the colophon are registered trademarks of Callisto Publishing LLC

All rights reserved. No part of this book may be reproduced in any form or by any electronic or mechanical means including information storage and retrieval systems—except in the case of brief quotations embodied in critical articles or reviews—without permission in writing from its publisher, Sourcebooks LLC.

All biblical verses are used as reflected in the King James version of the Christian Bible unless otherwise noted.

Published by Callisto Publishing LLC C/O Sourcebooks LLC
P.O. Box 4410, Naperville, Illinois 60567-4410
(630) 961-3900
callistopublishing.com

This product conforms to all applicable CPSC and CPSIA standards.

Source of Production: 1010 Printing Asia Limited, Kwun Tong, Hong Kong, China
Date of Production: March 2024
Run Number: 5038113

Printed and bound in China.
OGP 10 9 8 7 6 5 4 3 2 1

CONTENTS

Introduction v

How to Use This Book vi

Week 1: The Very Beginning 1
Week 2: Adam and Eve 4
Week 3: The First Brothers: Cain and Abel 7
Week 4: Noah Builds an Ark 10
Week 5: The Story of Job 13
Week 6: Abraham and Sarah Waited 17
Week 7: A Wife for Isaac 20
Week 8: Brothers at Odds 23
Week 9: Joseph Forgives 26
Week 10: Moses and the Burning Bush 30
Week 11: The Ten Commandments 33
Week 12: Joshua and the Fall of Jericho 36
Week 13: Deborah: Judge, Prophet, Warrior 40
Week 14: The Strength of Samson 43
Week 15: Naomi and Ruth: A Story of Faithfulness 46
Week 16: Samuel Hears God's Voice 49
Week 17: The Courage of David 52
Week 18: David Trusts God 55
Week 19: A Song of Thanksgiving to the Lord 59
Week 20: Solomon Seeks God's Wisdom 62
Week 21: Jonah: The Runaway Prophet 65
Week 22: Prophets of the Old Testament 68
Week 23: Shadrach, Meshach, and Abednego 71
Week 24: Daniel Faces the Lions' Den 74
Week 25: God's Purpose for Esther 77
Week 26: Nehemiah: A Man of Prayer 80

Week 27:	An Unexpected King	83
Week 28:	Elizabeth's Very Special Visitor	86
Week 29:	Jesus Is Born!	89
Week 30:	A Message from John the Baptist	92
Week 31:	Temptation in the Wilderness	95
Week 32:	Jesus Calls the Twelve Disciples	98
Week 33:	Feeding Five Thousand!	101
Week 34:	Jesus Calms the Storm	104
Week 35:	Nicodemus: A Curious Pharisee	107
Week 36:	Jesus: The Great Healer	110
Week 37:	Mary, Martha, and Jesus	113
Week 38:	A Good Neighbor	117
Week 39:	The Lost Son	120
Week 40:	Lazarus, Come Out!	123
Week 41:	Jesus Teaches Us How to Pray	126
Week 42:	Zacchaeus Finds Jesus	129
Week 43:	Jesus: The King	132
Week 44:	The Last Supper	135
Week 45:	Jesus in Gethsemane	138
Week 46:	Jesus Died and Lives Again!	141
Week 47:	Saul Sees the Light	144
Week 48:	A Miracle through Tabitha and Peter	147
Week 49:	The Disciples Share the Good News	150
Week 50:	What Will Heaven Be Like?	154
Week 51:	Put on the Armor of God	157
Week 52:	Faith that Saves	160

Answer Key   *163*

INTRODUCTION

Welcome to the *Bible Study Workbook for Kids*! I wrote this book as a mother who has always wanted to help her kids discover, understand, and love God's Word. My goal is for you (and your parents or guardians) to have accessible Bible stories, lessons, and supporting exercises to help you grow in your relationship with God.

This book is crafted with all these things in mind:

- It is written to you, but it is for your family to use together.
- It is written for parents to use as a resource to familiarize and engage their children in God's amazing Word.
- The story summaries do not cover every detail of every Bible story. Instead, each identifies a lesson that shows how God's plan is always perfect—for His glory, and for our good.
- The supporting exercises, object lessons, and discussion questions are designed to reinforce concepts and create opportunities for deeper conversations about God with everyone in the family.

I hope this book will give you wonderful opportunities for meaningful family time that fosters both spiritual growth and fun with one another!

HOW TO USE THIS BOOK

Inside are 52 lessons—26 from the Old Testament and 26 from the New Testament. The best way to use this book is to start at the beginning and complete one lesson and its activities each week. Here's what you'll find for each lesson:

Bible Lesson: This includes scripture references, a theme, a summary, and God's message. Read the scriptures using the biblical translation of your choice. This is important, since the summary is only an overview of the story. Read the theme, then discuss with your parent or guardian how God's message connects the story with our present lives.

Exercise: This is an on-the-page activity to help you learn more about the story and its message.

Object Lesson: This is a little hands-on fun to reinforce learning. You should have everything you need to do the activity at home. Feel free to make substitutions based on what you have at home and feel comfortable using.

Discuss It: These conversation starters provide an opportunity for teaching and reinforcing God's Word. You can use the lines on the page to write your answers or discuss them out loud with your parent or guardian.

I pray God blesses your time as you go through this book. What a privilege it is to learn about the loving truth of God's Word!

WEEK 1:
The Very Beginning

SCRIPTURE REFERENCE: Genesis 1–2:2
THEME: God created everything out of nothing

The Story: This is the first story in the Bible and our first look at God and His love for us. Before Earth existed, there was nothing—except God! There were no birds, no sun, no wind, and no internet. In six days, God made our world and everything in it, and He made it all from nothing. He even showed us how to rest on the seventh day after six days of hard work. Pretty cool, right?

God's Message: This story shows us God's awesome power, creativity, glory, goodness, and great love for us. He created everything we need, but He also made things just because He knew we would like them. God could have created one type of flower, but instead He made hundreds of thousands in every color and shape. God could have made all people the same, but He didn't. Isn't it amazing how creative God was starting with nothing?

UNSCRAMBLE IT!

Read Genesis 1–2:2 and unscramble the words to complete the sentences. One or two letters have been included to help!

1. **TLHIG** On the first day, God said, "Let there be | l | i | g | h | t |." (Genesis 1:3)

2. **TIFHF** God made the creatures of the sea and creatures that fly on the | f | i | f | t | y | day. (Genesis 1:21–23)

3. **RTAWSE** On day two, God separated the | w | a | t | e | r | s | and called it sky. (Genesis 1:6–8)

4. **TSALPN** God made the land, seas, | p | l | a | n | t | s |, and trees on day three. (Genesis 1:11–13)

5. **EASS** God named the water under the sky | s | e | a | s |. (Genesis 1:10)

6. **TFURHO** The | f | o | u | r | t | h | day is when God set the sun and moon. (Genesis 1:16–19)

7. **GAMEI** On the sixth day, God made mankind in His own | i | m | a | g | e |. (Genesis 1:27)

8. **DEESRT** On day seven, God | r | e | s | t | e | d |. (Genesis 2:2)

(See page 163 for answers)

2 BIBLE STUDY WORKBOOK FOR KIDS

CREATION CHALLENGE

Materials:

clay or play dough
timer

Let's see how creative YOU are!

Directions: Set the timer for one minute. Make anything you want with your clay before the timer goes off. You might make a pet, a person, or a star. Make a new one-minute creation as many times as you'd like.

Lesson: When God created Earth and everything in it, He made it out of nothing. He also made us all different. Are your creations the same or different? What could you create with other things, like leaves, sand, or snow? Genesis 1:27 says we are made in God's image. You can see God's creativity in your own unique creations.

DISCUSS IT!

God created everything out of nothing. What words would you use to describe God?

You are made in God's image. What does that mean to you?

WEEK 1: THE VERY BEGINNING

WEEK 2:
Adam and Eve

SCRIPTURE REFERENCE: Genesis 2–3
THEME: Sin makes things messy

The Story: God created the first man, Adam, and the first woman, Eve, on the sixth day. They lived with God in the beautiful Garden of Eden. God let them eat from every tree in the garden, except one—the tree of the knowledge of good and evil. One day, the serpent asked Eve, "Did God really say to not eat from that one tree?" The serpent caused Eve to question God, and both Eve and Adam ate from the tree. This was the first sin and the reason God sent Adam and Eve out of the garden.

God's Message: Sin broke Adam and Eve's perfect relationship with God. Since then, all of us have sinned, and we all are separated from God, but there is good news! God loves us so much He sent us His only son, Jesus! Sin still makes things messy, but through Jesus, God made a way to heal what was broken.

QUICK QUIZ

Circle the correct answer to each question in the quiz.

1. What creature deceived Eve?

    a. a serpent
    b. a spider
    c. a lizard

2. What is the name of the tree God said not to eat from?

    a. tree of life
    b. tree of the knowledge of good and evil
    c. tree of help and friendship

3. What part of Adam did God use to make Eve?

    a. a tooth
    b. a rib
    c. a hair

4. What is the name of the garden?

    a. Garden of Gethsemane
    b. Botanical Garden
    c. Garden of Eden

5. What did God do when He discovered Adam and Eve's sin?

    a. made them clothes and banished them
    b. sent them to sit under a tree and think about what they did
    c. made them do chores in the garden

6. Who did God give to us to save us from our sins?

    a. Jesus
    b. Moses
    c. Abraham

(See page 163 for answers)

SIN MAKES A MESS

Materials:

tube of toothpaste
paper plate

Let's see why it's important to listen to God and trust His Word!

Directions: Squeeze an inch of toothpaste onto the plate. Then try to clean up the toothpaste by putting it back into the tube.

Lesson: Sin makes a mess! Adam and Eve's disobedience, or sin, separated them from God. We cannot put the toothpaste back in the tube, just like we can't undo the effect sin has on our lives and the lives of others. The good news is we have a savior, Jesus, who came to make things right.

DISCUSS IT!

Read Romans 3:23. Adam and Eve committed the first sin, but who else has sinned?

_____

_____

Read John 3:16. What does that verse tell us about God's plan to fix the mess caused by sin?

_____

_____

WEEK 3:
The First Brothers: Cain and Abel

SCRIPTURE REFERENCE: Genesis 4
THEME: God shows mercy

The Story: Adam and Eve's first two sons were Cain and Abel. One day, the brothers offered gifts to God. Cain brought gifts from his crops while Abel brought gifts from his flock of sheep. God preferred Abel's gift. This made Cain so angry that he killed his brother! Because of Cain's terrible sin, God sent him away from his home. However, though Cain sinned, God showed him mercy by placing a special mark on him so people would know he was under God's protection. If someone killed Cain, God would punish that person seven times over.

God's Message: Sin separated Cain from his family and home. God takes sin seriously, and He shows us how sin makes everything worse than doing the right thing. Though Cain deserved serious consequences for his awful sin, God showed amazing mercy to him. This is an example of the love and mercy God gives to each one of us.

WRITE IT ON YOUR HEART!

Cain let jealousy and anger drive his actions. His sin was awful, but God sees all sin as awful. A wonderful way to keep sin from our hearts is to know God. How can we know God? By knowing His Word, the Bible, and filling our hearts with its truth.

Write the verses in the heart shapes below and challenge your family to memorize them with you!

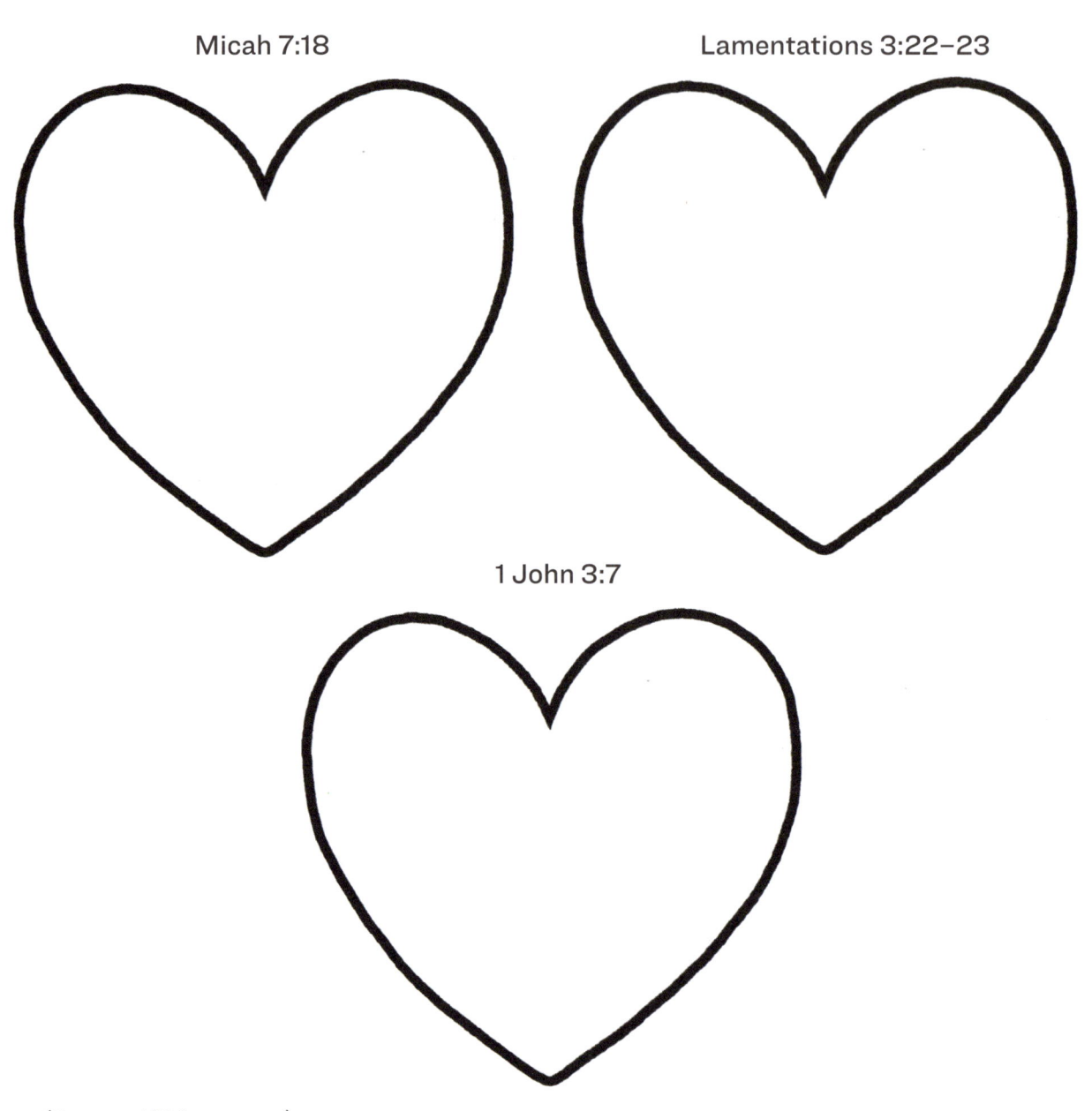

Micah 7:18

Lamentations 3:22–23

1 John 3:7

(See page 163 for answers)

GOD'S MERCY NEVER ENDS!

Materials:

large bowl of water
empty bowl
water dropper or ⅛ teaspoon

Let's see how God's mercy never ends!

Directions: Fill the big bowl with water. Use the water dropper (or teaspoon) to move the water to the empty bowl. Will you have the patience and energy to move all the water one drop at a time?

Lesson: Moving all the water from the full bowl to the empty bowl feels like it will take forever, doesn't it? That is like God's mercy for us. It is forever! He drops His mercy on our lives over and over again, except the bowl of His mercy will never empty!

DISCUSS IT!

Does God stay angry forever? Why does God give us mercy?

Does God want you to show mercy? What are two different ways you can show mercy when you feel frustrated or jealous?

WEEK 3: THE FIRST BROTHERS: CAIN AND ABEL

WEEK 4:
Noah Builds an Ark

SCRIPTURE REFERENCE: Genesis 6:9–9:17
THEME: Be obedient to God

The Story: After God made the world, people multiplied and covered the earth. Unfortunately, those people were always disobeying God. This made God very sad, but there was one man who still loved God and obeyed him—Noah. God gave Noah very detailed directions to build a huge boat, called an ark. God told Noah He was going to flood the earth. The ark would save Noah's family along with at least two of every kind of animal.

God's Message: Everyone thought Noah was crazy to build a big boat in the middle of the desert, but Noah obeyed God. He understood that not obeying God is sinful. Just as God promised, the rains came and water flooded the earth. Because Noah was obedient, his family and the animals on board the ark were saved.

WEEK 5:
The Story of Job

SCRIPTURE REFERENCE: Job 1–2:12; 27:1-6; 42:10-17
THEME: God rewards the faithful

The Story: Job lived a life that pleased God. Satan (the devil) told God that Job was only faithful because his life was so good, but God knew Job loved Him and was faithful to Him. God allowed Satan to test Job's faith. Job lost his riches and his family and got very sick. Job remained faithful through it all, and in the end, God blessed Job many times over and gave him twice as much as he had before. God also gave Job more children and he lived so long he got to see his great-grandchildren, and even his great-great-grandchildren!

God's Message: It's hard to read about someone who is sad or in pain, especially when we know that God allowed it. We don't always understand God's plan. Like Job, we need to remember that God is good and has a plan for us and will reward us for being faithful.

WHO WAS JOB?

What kind of man was Job? List his qualities here (Job 1:1):

List all the things Job lost (Job 1:14–19):

How did Job react to losing these things? (Job 1:20)

Draw a picture of how Job reacted to the awful news and write a caption for it.

You've written a lot! Take a second and shake out your hands. Now write one more thing, verse 1:22 in Job. Read it out loud when you are done!

(See page 163 for answers)

WEEK 5: THE STORY OF JOB

LIFE CAN BE A PUZZLE

Material:

small puzzle (fewer than 24 pieces)

Let's see how hard it is to understand when you can't see the whole picture.

Directions: Place the puzzle pieces on a table but keep them all upside down! It is going to be extra hard, but try your best to put the puzzle together with the pieces upside down.

Lesson: Doing a puzzle is hard when you don't have the picture to help you, but you know that there's a plan thanks to the picture on the box. Thinking about God's plan for you can be like doing this puzzle, knowing there's a perfect picture on the other side.

DISCUSS IT!

How do you talk to God when you are sad or hurting?

Think of a time something didn't go your way. Do you believe that God loved you even then?

WEEK 6:
Abraham and Sarah Waited

SCRIPTURE REFERENCE: Genesis 15:1–6; 17:15–19; 21:1–6
THEME: God rewards patience

The Story: The Bible is full of strong people who trusted God, but even they had to learn to wait. In Genesis, we read about Abraham and Sarah, who had to wait a very, very long time to have a child. How long? Abraham was 75 years old when God promised he and his wife Sarah a son. Seventy-five is a pretty old age to have a baby, but their son Isaac wasn't born until Sarah was 90 and Abraham was 100 years old. They waited 25 years for God's promise!

God's Message: Even though Abraham and Sarah were very old when God made His promise, Abraham trusted that God would keep His promise to give them a son. The next time you must wait, even when it's hard, think of Abraham and Sarah, who trusted God and had to learn to wait, just like you.

WAITING PRACTICE

In each of the first blank spaces below, write examples of times when it was hard for you to wait. In the second blank, write something you've done in that situation that didn't show patience. In the last blank, write down what you can try to do instead the next time it's hard for you to be patient. The first one is filled out for you.

When **_standing in line_**, instead of **_poking my neighbor_**, I will **_keep my hands to myself_**.

When _____, instead of _____

_____, I will _____.

When _____, instead of _____

_____, I will _____.

When _____, instead of _____

_____, I will _____.

(See page 163 for answers)

18 BIBLE STUDY WORKBOOK FOR KIDS

TURNING WATER INTO ICE

Materials:

water
ice tray or plastic bottle
freezer

Let's practice patience by waiting for ice to freeze!

Directions: Fill the ice tray or bottle with water. If using a bottle, put on the lid. Place the ice tray or bottle in the freezer and wait for the water to freeze.

Lesson: Just as we know water will turn to ice in the freezer, we also know God keeps His promises! Water does not turn into ice right away, but we know it will. How long does it take? Five minutes? One hundred minutes? We have to be patient!

DISCUSS IT!

What is the longest you have waited for something? Was it easy to wait?

Does it help to know about great people of the Bible who also struggled to wait? Why or why not?

WEEK 6: ABRAHAM AND SARAH WAITED

WEEK 7:
A Wife for Isaac

SCRIPTURE REFERENCE: Genesis 24
THEME: God answers prayer

The Story: Abraham sent a servant to his homeland to find a wife for his son Isaac. The servant made the journey and stopped at a well for water. He prayed that God would send Isaac's future wife to the same well. God did send a woman. When she drew water for the servant and for his camels, he knew she was sent by God! Her name was Rebekah, and her family knew God had planned for them to meet. Rebekah returned with the servant and married Isaac, who loved her very much.

God's Message: There is a reason the Bible has many stories that show how God answers prayer. Imagine making a long journey in the desert without a map or a phone to call the people you were going to visit! The servant prayed and the Lord answered, and it was clear to everyone God was at work.

DIG INTO THE DETAILS

Let's learn more about the details in the story of Isaac and Rebekah. Read Genesis 24 and 25. Then draw a line to connect each statement with its answer.

1. Isaac's father's name (Genesis 24:1–4)

2. Abraham sent a servant to find this for Isaac. (Genesis 24:4)

3. The number of camels the servant took with him (Genesis 24:10)

4. Where the servant met Rebekah (Genesis 24:15–16)

5. The servant prayed that Rebekah would give water to him, and these also. (Genesis 24:14)

6. Jewelry that the servant gave Rebekah (Genesis 24:22)

7. Rebekah's brother's name (Genesis 24:50)

8. Isaac's age when he married Rebekah (Genesis 25:20)

a well/spring

Laban

40

10

gold bracelets

Abraham

his camels

a wife

Extra credit! Read Genesis 25:19–26. What were the names of Isaac and Rebekah's two sons?

(See page 163 for answers)

WEEK 7: A WIFE FOR ISAAC

JUST A CALL AWAY

Material:

phone

Let's think about how God answers prayer.

Directions: With an adult's permission, call someone (maybe a grandparent or other adult you respect). Make a plan to get together or ask them about their day.

Lesson: Prayer is like calling someone who loves us. We can't see the person we call, but we trust they hear us and will answer when we speak to them. God answered exactly as Abraham's servant asked, but God won't always give us exactly what we ask for. We must trust that He will always listen and give an answer that is for our best and for His glory.

DISCUSS IT!

Do you believe God hears your prayers? What are two things you prayed to God about today?

_____

_____

Read Philippians 4:6–7. What do you think He is telling us about prayer?

_____

_____

WEEK 8:
Brothers at Odds

SCRIPTURE REFERENCE: Genesis 25:19–34; 27:1–45; 33:1–4
THEME: God uses all things for good

The Story: Esau and Jacob were twin brothers. Esau was born first, which meant he should be the one to get a special blessing from their father, Isaac. Jacob and Rebekah, the twins' mother, tricked Isaac into giving the blessing to Jacob instead. Esau was so angry that Jacob had to leave home until his brother calmed down. Many years later, the brothers forgave each other because they realized God had a plan.

God's Message: God never wants us to allow sin in our lives. Lying is sin. Jacob and Rebekah's lie caused Esau's anger—the reason Jacob had to leave his home. The consequence of their sin caused hurt in the family, but God loved the brothers and had a plan for them. God works all things for good for those He has called and loves.

DIFFERENCES BETWEEN BROTHERS

Jacob and Esau were very different from each other. Draw a picture of each brother. Then list a few interesting facts about each brother using Genesis 25:19-34, 27:1–45.

ESAU	JACOB

(See page 164 for answers)

24 BIBLE STUDY WORKBOOK FOR KIDS

MAKING SOMETHING GOOD

Materials:

your favorite cookie recipe
recipe ingredients

Let's see how yucky things can be made into something good.

Directions: With an adult's help, bake a batch of your favorite cookies. While mixing the ingredients, taste the butter, baking soda, and salt. They don't taste good on their own. Once the cookies are baked, enjoy how the ingredients came together to make something yummy.

Lesson: Baking is kind of messy, and not every ingredient tastes good. But after the mess, when everything is mixed together, there is a good result—cookies! Life with God is like baking. He takes the messy ingredients of our lives and uses them for good.

DISCUSS IT!

How does this story show that God can fix a bad situation?

God makes things good, but does that mean there is no consequence for sin?

WEEK 9:
Joseph Forgives

SCRIPTURE REFERENCE: Genesis 37; 39–47:11
THEME: Be willing to forgive

The Story: Jacob had twelve sons and one daughter. He loved them all, but Joseph was his favorite. When he gave Joseph a fancy robe, it made his brothers really jealous. Later, Joseph told his brothers about a dream where they bowed down to him. The angry brothers sold him into slavery. Eventually, the king of Egypt, Pharaoh, chose Joseph to be a leader because he was wise. Joseph's powerful position helped him save Egypt from a great famine. He forgave his brothers and was able to save his family, too.

God's Message: God's plan is not always clear when bad things happen. If Joseph had not been sent to Egypt, Pharaoh could not have given him a position to save people during a time of famine. Joseph didn't let anger win. Instead, he showed honor serving God and Egypt, and showed forgiveness and mercy to his brothers.

CHOOSING THE RIGHT WORDS

Circle the word that fits each sentence. You can use a dictionary if you need to.

1. Joseph's brothers were (jealous, excited) that he got a special coat from his father.

2. (Forgiveness, Bitterness) is what God wants us to have in our hearts.

3. Joseph showed his brothers (cruelty, mercy) when they came to him in Egypt.

4. (The Governor, Pharaoh) had a dream that Joseph helped him understand.

5. Joseph was made second-in-command in Egypt because he was (good-looking, wise).

6. Joseph saved Egypt from (an invasion, a famine).

7. Joseph's forgiveness for his brothers caused him to (struggle, prosper).

(See page 164 for answers)

continued

WEEK 9: JOSEPH FORGIVES 27

Choosing the Right Words *continued*

Draw a picture below of what you think Joseph's fancy robe may have looked like.

LIKE A SHINY PENNY

Materials:

old penny
eraser

Let's see how forgiveness helps us show God's love.

Directions: Rub the eraser on the penny to clean it. Really scrub! This will take some time, especially if the penny is very dirty, but work on getting that penny clean and shiny!

Lesson: That old, dirty penny is like a heart that is unforgiving. The eraser represents God's forgiveness. It takes some time and effort, but when we work to obey God and forgive others, we become like a shiny penny and can show God's love to those around us.

DISCUSS IT!

Joseph forgave his brothers when they did something awful to him. Talk about a time when you had to forgive someone who hurt you.

Do you think that even if you struggle to forgive, God can still make things good?

WEEK 9: JOSEPH FORGIVES

WEEK 10:
Moses and the Burning Bush

SCRIPTURE REFERENCE: Exodus 3–4
THEME: God helps the ones He calls

The Story: One day, Moses saw something strange—a burning bush that talked! The Lord spoke to him from inside the bush. God told Moses He was going to use him to save the Israelites from Egypt. Moses understood it would be hard work and didn't think he would be able to do it. He gave God reasons why He should choose somebody else. But God knew Moses and provided everything he needed to do the job He was asking him to do.

God's Message: Moses didn't think he could do the job God wanted him to do, but God knew Moses and knew he could do as He asked. God knows you, too! Sometimes we don't feel like we can do what God wants, but just like Moses, God knows us and will give us the knowledge and ability we need to do what He asks of us.

FILL IN THE BLANKS

Learn a little bit more about Moses's life before the burning bush and after. Pick the correct word from the word bank to complete each sentence. You can check the verses if you get stuck.

1. Pharaoh ordered that every Hebrew baby _____ be killed. (Exodus 1:22)

2. Moses's mother placed him in a _____ in the river. (Exodus 2:1–3)

3. Pharaoh's _____ found the baby in the river. (Exodus 2:5–6)

4. An angel of the Lord appeared to Moses in a burning _____. (Exodus 3:2)

5. God punished Egypt with ten _____. (Exodus 7–11)

6. God passed over the houses of the _____. (Exodus 12:27)

7. The Israelites crossed the _____ Sea. (Exodus 14:22)

8. Pharaoh's horses, chariots, and horsemen were covered by the _____. (Exodus 15)

WORD BANK

Red	sea	plagues
bush	boy	daughter
Israelites	basket	

(See page 164 for answers)

WEEK 10: MOSES AND THE BURNING BUSH 31

HEARING GOD'S CALL

Materials:

brown, white, yellow, and orange construction paper
glue
scissors
black marker or crayon

Let's think about how we hear God's voice.

Directions: Cut the brown paper into a dozen (or more) strips. Glue the strips onto the white construction paper so they look like a bush's sticks. Cut out six to eight orange and yellow flame shapes and glue them to the sticks. On each flame, write a way God speaks to us (for example, through parents, prayer, or God's Word).

Lesson: God probably won't use a burning bush to speak to you, but God does communicate with us. We just have to listen.

DISCUSS IT!

Have you ever made an excuse for why you couldn't do something? Do we ever make excuses to God?

Write about a hard job you had to do and how you handled it.

WEEK 11:
The Ten Commandments

SCRIPTURE REFERENCE: Exodus 20:1–17, 1 Peter 1:13–16
THEME: Do your best to be holy

The Story: A few months after Moses led the Israelites out of Egypt, they came to Mount Sinai. Moses went to the top of the mountain to speak with God. There, God gave Moses a message to share with His children. God's message was carved on two tablets. Can you guess what was on those tablets? The Ten Commandments!

God's Message: God wants His people to be holy. He didn't leave us on Earth to guess how we should live. After God saved the Israelites, He gave them clear instructions on how to live a holy life. Many Bible stories show us how sin separates us from God. The Ten Commandments are clear about what God's people can do to stay close to Him and how to live holy lives. God has never left His people without His wisdom and help.

GOD'S RULES

What are the Ten Commandments? Read Exodus 20:1–17 and summarize each commandment on the tablets below.

1.
2.
3.
4.
5.

6.
7.
8.
9.
10.

(See page 164 for answers)

STAYING ON TRACK

Materials:

plate with little to no rim
deep bowl
a marble

Let's see how God's instructions help keep us holy.

Directions: Place the marble on the plate and try to make it spin around the plate. What happens? Now place the marble in the bowl and make it spin around inside. Does it act differently?

Lesson: Living without God's instructions is like being the marble on the plate. The marble does whatever it wants—and it really doesn't want to stay on the plate! The sides of the bowl represent God's commandments. They help keep us from sinning and going off track, which separates us from God.

DISCUSS IT!

What does "holy" mean? What does it mean for you to live a holy life?

Why is it important to God that we learn to live a holy life?

WEEK 12:
Joshua and the Fall of Jericho

SCRIPTURE REFERENCE: Joshua 1; 5:13–6:27
THEME: God blesses those who obey Him

The Story: After Moses died, God made Joshua the leader of the Israelites. God told Joshua to lead the Israelites to the promised land—a new, beautiful home for His people. The city of Jericho, a city in the land of Canaan, with its big walls, was in their path. Canaanite people were a whole land of people against God who did many horrible things. God told Joshua to command the army and priests to march around Jericho for seven days to make the walls come down. Though it felt like an odd plan, Joshua obeyed, and the walls of Jericho fell!

God's Message: God used Joshua to show us the power and blessing of obedience. God asked Joshua to tell the Israelites to do things that didn't make sense to them, but Joshua showed trust in God's plan. In turn, God blessed Joshua and the Israelites for their faith and obedience. We see God's blessings when we obey, as the Bible shows us over and over.

BUILDING ON OBEDIENCE

Read John 14:15 and write the verse here:

_____

_____

_____

Read Ephesians 6:1. What does it say about obeying your parents?

_____

_____

_____

What did Jesus say about obedience in Luke 11:28?

_____

_____

_____

(See page 164 for answers)

continued

WEEK 12: JOSHUA AND THE FALL OF JERICHO

Building on Obedience *continued*

WAYS I CAN BE OBEDIENT:

To my parents:

At school:

For the Lord:

OBEY EVERY DAY

Materials:

piece of paper
marker
stickers

Let's practice being obedient!

Directions: Write O B E D I E N C E on the piece of paper with the marker. Each time you obey your parent or guardian, put a sticker on top of one of the letters. Every day, start with a new paper. Try to cover all the letters every day! When you have covered every letter every day for a week, enjoy a reward that is special to you or talk to your parent about how to decide on a reward together.

Lesson: Sometimes God will ask you to do something you don't want to do. You can learn how to obey God by practicing obedience in your family.

DISCUSS IT!

Is obeying always easy or is it often hard? Why or why not?

What did you learn about obedience in this story? Do you believe God's plan is always good?

WEEK 13:
Deborah: Judge, Prophet, Warrior

SCRIPTURE REFERENCE: Judges 4–5
THEME: You have a divine purpose

The Story: Deborah, a judge and prophetess, was a strong leader for Israel. She was wise and people went to her for advice. One day, God gave her a message for Barak, Israel's military commander. He was to fight Sisera, an evil enemy of Israel who was doing terrible things to God's people. Barak agreed to do it, but only if Deborah went with him. She did, and Sisera and his army were defeated.

God's Message: God saw that Deborah was wise and He chose her to lead the army of Israel to defeat its enemy. This story is a great lesson on how God can use any of us according to His purpose. Just as He did for Deborah, God has a perfect plan for every one of us. He will use your unique talents and strengths for His glory and your own good.

FILL IN THE BLANKS

Pick the correct word from the word bank to complete each sentence. You can check the verses if you get stuck.

1. Deborah the judge held court under the _____ of Deborah. (Judges 4:5)

2. Deborah was leading (or judging) _____ at the time. (Judges 4:4)

3. She was a judge and a _____. (Judges 4:4)

4. _____ said, "If you go with me, I will go." (Judges 4:8)

5. _____ killed Barak with a tent peg. (Judges 4:21)

6. _____ was the commander of Jabin's army. (Judges 4:2)

7. Jabin was the king of _____. (Judges 4:23)

8. Barak and Deborah sang praise to the _____. (Judges 5:2)

WORD BANK

Sisera	Lord	Canaan
prophet	Barak	Israel
Jael	Palm	

(See page 164 for answers)

WEEK 13: DEBORAH: JUDGE, PROPHET, WARRIOR

ARE YOU AN INFLUENCER?

Materials:

piece of paper
pencil

Let's see how God can use your life to affect other people.

Directions: Fold the paper in half. On one half, write down the people you see each day. They could be people you know, or people you see only in passing. On the other half, write ways you think you affect their lives (maybe you held the door open for someone). How is God using you to show His glory to others?

Lesson: Every time you meet someone, you have a chance to influence or touch their life for God! Think about how God can use you in the lives of people you meet.

DISCUSS IT!

What is the goal of God's plan? Who will He use to make it happen?

Have you ever felt like God wanted you to do something? What was it? Was it easy or hard?

WEEK 14:
The Strength of Samson

SCRIPTURE REFERENCE: Judges 13–16
THEME: God gives us our strength

The Story: The Philistines were enemies of God's people, the Israelites. God used a man named Samson to rescue them. Before Samson was born, the Lord told his mother to never cut his hair. It would be the source of his strength. Samson was so strong he didn't need an army for backup! During that time, Israelites were only allowed to spend time with other Israelites to keep their faith strong. But Samson fell in love with a Philistine woman named Delilah, who tricked him into telling her the secret to his strength. While he was sleeping, she cut off Samson's hair. When he woke up, his strength was gone!

God's Message: Samson lost God's protection when he told Delilah the secret of his strength, but in the end, God used him to save His people from the Philistines. In fact, Samson died saving the Israelites! We keep reading about imperfect leaders God used for His glory, but it wasn't until God sent Jesus that we finally got the perfect leader to save us all for eternity.

TEST YOURSELF!

Read Judges 13–16. Then test yourself and match each question with its answer.

1. ____ A person dedicated to God from birth (Judges 13:5)

2. ____ How many years did Samson lead Israel? (Judges 15:20)

3. ____ Ferocious animal Samson killed with his bare hands (Judges 14:5–6)

4. ____ Samson scooped out _____ from the lion's dead body. (Judges 14:8–9)

5. ____ She tricked Samson into telling her the secret of his strength. (Judges 16:4)

6. ____ Who was Samson's father? (Judges 13:2)

7. ____ When Samson pushed against the pillars, the _____ fell. (Judges 16:30)

8. ____ Samson married a _____ woman. (Judges 14:1–3)

9. ____ Samson told the wedding guests a _____. (Judges 14:12)

10. ____ Samson struck down 1,000 men with the _____ of a donkey. (Judges 15:15)

a. Delilah
b. Manoah
c. Nazirite
d. Philistine
e. twenty
f. riddle
g. jawbone
h. temple
i. lion
j. honey

(See page 165 for answers)

BIBLE STUDY WORKBOOK FOR KIDS

FOLLOW THE LEADER

Material:

2 or more people

Let's see how our leaders affect our lives.

Directions: Take turns being a leader and follower. The leader can lead the follower on a walk outside, explain how to draw a picture, or tell them how to make a sandwich! Use your imagination for ways to lead.

Lesson: Samson's unique leadership skill was his strength. What skills has God given you to lead others? When you were the leader, what did you help your followers experience? A leader can have a lot of power over those they lead, so it's important to be careful about what you lead them to do!

DISCUSS IT!

Read 1 Peter 2:21. Who is the perfect leader that God has given us to save us from our sin?

What are some unique things about you that God can use to help you be a leader?

WEEK 14: THE STRENGTH OF SAMSON

WEEK 15:
Naomi and Ruth: A Story of Faithfulness

SCRIPTURE REFERENCE: Ruth 1–4
THEME: God is faithful

The Story: Ruth was a Moabite woman who was married to one of Naomi's sons, an Israelite. Sadly, both of their husbands died while they were living in Moab. Ruth could have stayed with her family in Moab, but she left her homeland. She went to Israel, a place she did not know, with Naomi. While caring for Naomi, Ruth met and married Boaz. In Israel, God provided a home and family for Naomi and Ruth.

God's Message: Though Ruth could have stayed with her family, she chose to go with Naomi to support her mother-in-law. Both Ruth and Naomi loved God. They had trust in God's faithfulness, and God was faithful. He knew their needs and He provided. Just like with Ruth and Naomi, we don't always know what will happen, but we trust that God knows our needs and will be faithful to us, too!

RETELL THE STORY

Pick the correct word from the word bank to complete each sentence. You can check the verses if you get stuck.

1. Why did Naomi's family move to Moab from Bethlehem? (Ruth 1:1–2) _____

2. What are the names of the two sisters-in-law? (Ruth 1:4) _____ and _____

3. Which daughter-in-law stayed with Naomi? (Ruth 1:16–18) _____

4. What city did Naomi and Ruth return to? (Ruth 1:19) _____

5. What is the name Naomi wanted to be called because life had become so hard? (Ruth 1:20) _____

6. To get food for the women, what did Ruth pick from the fields? (Ruth 2:2) _____ _____

7. Who saw Ruth and invited her to gather grain in his fields with his workers? (Ruth 2:8) _____

WORD BANK

Bethlehem
a famine
leftover grain
Ruth and Orpah
Mara
Boaz
Ruth

(See page 165 for answers)

WEEK 15: NAOMI AND RUTH: A STORY OF FAITHFULNESS

STICKY WATER

Materials:

cup filled halfway with water
paper plate or index card wider than the opening of the cup

Let's see an example of how God's faithfulness sticks!

Directions: Place the paper plate (or card) on top of the cup of water. Hold the cup over a sink. Turn the cup upside down while firmly holding the paper plate on top. Now let go of the plate. The plate sticks!

Lesson: Like the water sticks to the plate (even when we're nervous that it won't), God's faithfulness sticks to us. Faithfulness means you do what you say you are going to do—and God sure does that! The Bible is full of stories that show His faithfulness.

DISCUSS IT!

How was God faithful to Ruth and Naomi? How has God been faithful to you?

_____

_____

Do you think it was easy for Ruth to follow Naomi? Have you ever had to do something that was hard?

_____

_____

Week 16: Samuel Hears God's Voice

SCRIPTURE REFERENCE: 1 Samuel 1–3
THEME: God knows your heart

The Story: A woman named Hannah prayed to God to have a son. She vowed that if she were to have a son, she would give him to the Lord. Later, her son Samuel was born. When Samuel was just a boy, Hannah took him to the tabernacle so he could be raised and trained by Eli, a priest. Samuel grew up with a love of God. One night, God spoke directly to him, and the boy was ready to listen. Samuel grew up to be one of the most faithful leaders of Israel for the Lord.

God's Message: Samuel heard God's own voice! Can you imagine hearing God's voice? God knew Samuel's heart. He spoke to Samuel because He knew that Samuel loved Him and would listen to His words. Imagine what God can do through you when you love and trust Him!

QUICK QUIZ

Circle the correct answer to each question in the quiz.

1. What two things did Hannah promise God she would do if she had a son? (1 Samuel 1:11)

    a. raise him in the church and eat vegetables every day
    b. give him to the Lord and never cut his hair
    c. give him to the Lord and read the Bible every day

2. How many children did Hannah have? (1 Samuel 2:20–21)

    a. 1
    b. 3
    c. 5

3. Where was Samuel sleeping when he heard God's voice? (1 Samuel 3:3)

    a. outside in a tent
    b. on the floor next to Eli
    c. in the house of the Lord

4. After God spoke to Samuel that night, was that the last time? (1 Samuel 3:19–21)

    a. yes
    b. no

5. Read Hebrews 1:1–2. Who speaks to us today?

(See page 165 for answers)

WHAT'S ON THE INSIDE?

Materials:

plain envelope
plain paper bag
6 strips of paper
colored markers or crayons

Let's see why what's on the inside is so important.

Directions: Decorate the bag with markers or crayons. On three strips of paper, write not-so-nice things like "mean words" and "lying." On the other three strips, write good things like "kindness" and "love." Put the not-so-nice word strips in the decorated bag and the strips with good words in the plain envelope.

Lesson: Both the inside and outside of these two items are very different. Which item looks like it would have the best stuff inside? Just like you know what's inside each package, God knows what's inside your heart. God doesn't care what's on the outside. It's what is on the inside that matters.

DISCUSS IT!

What does God look at when He looks in our hearts?

What can you do to be ready to answer God's call?

WEEK 16: SAMUEL HEARS GOD'S VOICE

WEEK 17:
The Courage of David

SCRIPTURE REFERENCE: 1 Samuel 17
THEME: Faith in God gives us strength

The Story: David was just a boy who tended sheep. Goliath was a giant warrior. He wore a metal helmet and body armor, and he carried a spear and javelin. David wore no armor. His only weapon was his slingshot and a few stones. David was small, but his faith in God was bigger than Goliath. Courageous David took down the giant with one stone thrown from his slingshot!

God's Message: God used a boy to defeat one of the toughest warriors ever. It was David's courage and faith in God—not his strength—that saved the Israelites from the Philistine army. There is no age limit when it comes to how God can use those who are faithful. Faith in God gives us all the strength and courage we need to do what God asks us to do.

DAVID OR GOLIATH?

Read 1 Samuel 16:11–17:51 to learn more about David and Goliath. Then write the letter that corresponds to each fact under the name of the person it describes.

- **a.** Philistine soldier
- **b.** Israelite shepherd boy
- **c.** youngest of the family
- **d.** a giant
- **e.** wore no armor
- **f.** played the lyre
- **g.** wore a bronze helmet and armor
- **h.** carried a javelin, sword, and spear
- **i.** carried five stones and a sling
- **j.** trusted God's power
- **k.** relied on his own power

David

Goliath

(See page 165 for answers)

WEEK 17: THE COURAGE OF DAVID

FILLED WITH GOD

Materials:

balloon filled with air
balloon filled with water
lighter (never use a lighter yourself)
an adult

Let's see how God provides strength.

Directions: Ask an adult to hold the flame of the lighter an inch or two under the balloon filled with air. What happens? Now ask them to hold the flame under the balloon filled with water. What happens?

Lesson: The balloon filled with water is like a heart filled with God. When our hearts are filled with faith in God, He gives us strength. We can stand up to hard things with courage knowing God will give us the strength to make it through.

DISCUSS IT!

Have you ever felt like being young means you are weak? What does this story tell you about your own strength in God?

Can you think of a time when you had to be courageous?

54 BIBLE STUDY WORKBOOK FOR KIDS

WEEK 18:
David Trusts God

SCRIPTURE REFERENCE: 1 Samuel 24; 26
THEME: Trust and obey the Lord

The Story: David knew Saul was chasing him and trying to hurt him. David also knew that hurting Saul would be a sin. God had forbidden him to harm Saul because Saul was chosen by God. Because of this, David spared Saul's life when Saul was trying to hurt him. When Saul saw that David trusted and obeyed God, he asked God for forgiveness. God kept David safe and forgave Saul for his sin.

God's Message: In this story, we see David's amazing trust in God's plan and promise. David would not touch Saul, even though Saul was a very dangerous threat to his life. David didn't let his fear stop him. He continued being obedient to God and trusted in His perfect plan. That is what God asks us to do every day.

GETTING TO KNOW DAVID

Circle the numbers of things that describe David:

1. He had faith in God.

2. He was a man of courage.

3. He wasn't sure about trusting God.

4. He prayed to God and obeyed Him.

If I could ask King David one question, it would be:

_____

_____

_____

Read David's Psalm 31:14, then write it here:

_____

_____

_____

David is known for defeating Goliath, but he is most known for being a great king of Israel.

Draw a picture of King David in the space below:

(See page 165 for answers)

WEEK 18: DAVID TRUSTS GOD

A TRUST TEST

Materials:

water
plastic zip-top bag
sharp, round pencil (not a hexagonal-shaped pencil)
an adult

Let's see how it can be hard to trust.

Directions: Fill the bag with water and seal it closed. Have an adult hold the bag and quickly jab the pencil through the entire bag. If you want to test how much trust you have in the adult holding the bag, have them hold it over your head before they jab it! Do you flinch?

Lesson: Sometimes our lives get poked with holes, too. We get hurt or lose an important game. Trusting that the bag won't leak is like trusting God. Even when it feels like everything is going wrong, God is there for us.

DISCUSS IT!

What would you have done if you were David?

_____

_____

How should you treat those who are kind to you? What about those who are mean?

_____

_____

WEEK 19:
A Song of Thanksgiving to the Lord

SCRIPTURE REFERENCE: Psalm 107
THEME: Be thankful to the Lord

The Story: David trusted God and had faith in Him, but his life was not easy! The Book of Psalms is a collection of songs David wrote to God. Psalm 107 describes people who call out to God while they are struggling and in pain, and how God rescues them. David thanks the Lord and praises His goodness.

God's Message: Psalm 107 starts with "Give thanks to the Lord, for he is good." Remember how David had to run for his life—twice? Remember how he stood up to scary Goliath? If anyone had a right to complain about hard stuff, it would be David. Despite those many hard things, he praised God and gave Him glory. The entire Book of Psalms reminds us that God is good, and He is there for us.

PSALMS OF THANKFULNESS

Look up the verses below and write them on the lines.

Psalm 7:17

Psalm 106:1

The Book of Psalms is not the only place in the Bible that reminds us of God's goodness and how it's important to thank Him! What do the verses below say? Write them on the lines.

1 Timothy 4:4

1 Thessalonians 5:18

Now look at each verse you wrote. Circle all the words that include "**thank**" in them. Put a box around words that say God is **good**, **great**, or **righteous**.

(See page 165 for answers)

THANKFULNESS PRACTICE

Materials:

empty box
5 or 6 small items from around the house

Let's practice thankfulness.

Directions: Collect small items from around the house and place them into the box. Then come together as a family and get ready to practice. Take one item at a time from the box and take turns sharing why you are thankful for it.

Lesson: You can be thankful for a dead battery because it gave power to something you played with. You can be thankful for a dirty sock because it kept your foot clean and dry. Sometimes we might have to work at thankfulness, but we can always be thankful to God, for He is good!

DISCUSS IT!

Besides God, who else can you share your thankfulness with?

_____

_____

What are three things you can thank the Lord for today?

_____

_____

WEEK 20:
Solomon Seeks God's Wisdom

SCRIPTURE REFERENCE: 1 Kings 3:3–15
THEME: God's wisdom is a great gift

The Story: Solomon became the king of Israel after his father, David. Solomon knew it was a big responsibility, and he knew he could not be a good ruler on his own. Solomon prayed to God for help. He asked God for wisdom as a king and ruler. God did not ignore Solomon's prayer. In fact, God spoke to him in a dream. He told Solomon He was impressed he did not ask for a long life, riches, or victory over his enemies. God blessed Solomon with greater wisdom than anyone who ever lived.

God's Message: God told Solomon that if he followed His commands, He would not only give him wisdom as a ruler, but wisdom about many things! God honored Solomon's desire for wisdom, and many say he was the wisest man to ever live. Solomon did not become wise on his own. His wisdom came from the Lord!

QUICK QUIZ

Circle the correct answer to each question in the quiz.

1. When God said to Solomon in a dream, "Ask for whatever you want," what did Solomon ask for?

    a. long life
    b. riches
    c. wisdom
    d. victory in war

2. Read 1 Kings 3:28. Where did the people think Solomon's wisdom came from?

    a. himself
    b. God
    c. his dog
    d. books

3. Did the Lord give Solomon only the wisdom he asked for? What else did God give him?

    a. a new chariot
    b. a new scepter to impress everybody
    c. riches and honor
    d. lots of land

4. According to James 1:5, if anyone lacks wisdom they should:

    a. read more books
    b. ask God for more wisdom
    c. search the internet
    d. eat more spinach

What did David tell Solomon about seeking the Lord in 1 Chronicles 28:9?

(See page 165 for answers)

SOAK UP GOD'S WISDOM

Materials:

dry sponge
squirt gun or spray bottle filled with water
sink or bowl

Let's see why it's important to soak up God's wisdom!

Directions: Squirt the dry sponge with the squirt gun until it is soaked through. When the sponge is totally soaked, squeeze it out over the sink or bowl.

Lesson: The dry sponge is like us without God's wisdom. The water represents God's wisdom. When we pray (or squirt the water) God fills us with His wisdom. If we don't seek God's wisdom, we won't have it to use in our lives and the lives of others when we need it.

DISCUSS IT!

What might you need wisdom for?

_____

_____

Is there someone in your life who is wise? How did they become wise?

_____

_____

64 BIBLE STUDY WORKBOOK FOR KIDS

WEEK 21:
Jonah: The Runaway Prophet

SCRIPTURE REFERENCE: Jonah 1–3
THEME: Follow God's directions

The Story: God told the prophet Jonah to go to the city of Nineveh to preach against its wickedness. Jonah didn't want to go! Instead of following God's directions, Jonah ran away. He tried to escape on a boat, but God found Jonah and sent a terrible storm. The crew threw him overboard, and Jonah ended up in the belly of a very big fish. When he prayed to God for forgiveness and promised to go to Nineveh, God rescued him from the fish.

God's Message: Jonah thought running away from God would mean he wouldn't have to obey God. Can you imagine trying to run from God? Throughout the Bible, we see that God's plan is always good. In this story, we learn that not following God's directions affects others and won't stop God's plan.

PICTURE JONAH'S STORY

If you were stuck inside a fish, what would your prayer be?

_____

_____

Use the space below to draw part of Jonah's story. Some ideas include Jonah in the ship during the storm, Jonah inside a great fish, or the King of Nineveh described in Jonah 3:6.

(See page 165 for answers)

66 BIBLE STUDY WORKBOOK FOR KIDS

THE GELATIN TEST

Materials:

- 2 small boxes of instant gelatin dessert, like Jell-O
- saucepan
- water
- 2 bowls

Let's see how following directions can lead to good things!

Directions: With a parent's help, make one box of the gelatin dessert following the directions exactly. Make the other box but triple the water. Put both bowls in the refrigerator until the mixtures are set. How did they turn out? Enjoy the gelatin made according to the directions as a treat, and the other can be enjoyed as punch!

Lesson: God's plan is like the bowl of gelatin made from the directions. The dessert is jiggly and perfect! But when we stray from the directions, things don't end up like the picture on the box.

DISCUSS IT!

Do you feel like running away and hiding when your parents ask you to do something? Why or why not?

What big lesson did you learn from Jonah's story?

WEEK 22:
Prophets of the Old Testament

SCRIPTURE REFERENCE: 2 Peter 1:20–21, Deuteronomy 18:18–19
THEME: God speaks through prophets

The Story: Prophets are people God used to send his messages, and they never spoke their own opinions. God used prophets to speak to all people, not just those who believed in Him. God's prophets loved God. There are 16 books in the Old Testament that are written by prophets, but not every prophet had their own book.

God's Message: Prophets were both men and women God used to teach, warn, and guide people to God. When Adam and Eve were banished from the Garden of Eden, it meant that people could no longer walk and talk beside God in a perfect place. Instead, God used prophets to tell people of His love, send warnings, and speak His commands. God also used prophets to tell us about the coming of Jesus!

WHAT DID THE PROPHETS HEAR?

Look up and read each verse in the first column. Draw a line from the verse to the prophet it is speaking about, or to the prophet who wrote the verse. Then look at the third column. Draw a line from the name of the prophet in the center column to the matching line of words in the third column.

Exodus 3:1–4	Moses	ran from the Lord
Daniel 2:19	Deborah	saw a windstorm in a vision
Ezekiel 1:4	Abraham	saw three men (angels) standing nearby
Isaiah 6:8	Jonah	foretold Jesus would be born in Bethlehem
Genesis 18:2	Samuel	a mystery was revealed in a vision
1 Samuel 3:4–5	Isaiah	said, "Here I am."
Judges 4:9	Daniel	said, "I will go with you."
Numbers 12:10	Ezekiel	skin turned white
Jonah 1:3	Micah	saw a burning bush
Micah 5:2	Miriam	said, "Send me!"

(See pages 165–166 for answers)

WEEK 22: PROPHETS OF THE OLD TESTAMENT

HEAR GOD THROUGH THE DISTRACTIONS

Materials:

radio
Bible

God's Word is God's voice. Let's see why God's Word is important.

Directions: Turn on the radio. You may need to go to your family car for this, in which case, make sure to ask an adult to help you. Listen for a minute or two to several different stations. What do you hear?

Lesson: Maybe you heard music, the news, a commercial or two, or people sharing their opinions. That's a lot of noise and information to think through. Now open your Bible to 2 Timothy 3:16–17 and read those verses. The radio represents the noise and distraction of the world, but God's Word has all we need to hear Him.

DISCUSS IT!

Can you name a few of the prophets? Who is your favorite?

Why do you think God used prophets? What book does God use to speak to us today?

WEEK 23:
Shadrach, Meshach, and Abednego

SCRIPTURE REFERENCE: Daniel 3
THEME: Be brave and courageous in the Lord

The Story: King Nebuchadnezzar of Babylon made a huge statue of himself covered with gold. He ordered everyone to bow down and worship it. Anyone who did not worship the statue would be thrown into a fiery furnace! Three young men, Shadrach, Meshach, and Abednego, loved the Lord and refused to worship the statue. Nebuchadnezzar sent them to the fiery furnace—but they were not harmed! Not even one hair on their heads was burned. The king praised God and made the young men leaders in Babylon.

God's Message: Shadrach, Meshach, and Abednego did a very hard thing. They remained faithful to God knowing they could be killed for it. God used their faithfulness for His glory. King Nebuchadnezzar and his people saw with their own eyes how they stood for their God and how their God saved them. Through Shadrach, Meshach, and Abednego's brave faith, God was glorified!

QUICK QUIZ

Circle the correct answer to each question in the quiz.

1. Which king had a gold-covered statue made?

   a. David
   b. Saul
   c. Nebuchadnezzar

2. How did Shadrach, Meshach, and Abednego disobey the king?

   a. They fell asleep during his speech.
   b. They refused to worship the king's statue.
   c. They didn't eat all their dinner.

3. How did the king punish the three young men?

   a. They were thrown into a fiery furnace.
   b. They were put in time-out.
   c. They didn't get dessert at the banquet.

4. What did the king see when he looked into the furnace?

   a. three men
   b. four men
   c. a praise band

5. What did the king say when he saw the three young men were alive?

   a. That was WILD!
   b. What's your secret, guys?
   c. No other god can save in this way!

6. What happened to Shadrach, Meshach, and Abednego after they came out of the furnace?

   a. They were taken to the hospital.
   b. They were given important jobs.
   c. They took a long nap.

(See page 166 for answers)

FLOATING IN FAITH

Materials:

an orange
pitcher of water

Let's see how faith in God is like a layer of protection.

Directions: Take the orange and put it in the pitcher of water. What does the orange do? Now remove it from the water, peel it, and place it back into the pitcher. What does the orange do now?

Lesson: The orange peel represents faith. Just like the orange without a peel sinks to the bottom, we sink without faith. The next time you feel tempted to question God, remember the orange with the peel and float safely in God's love for you! When you're done with the experiment, eat the orange and talk about what you learned.

DISCUSS IT!

From where did Shadrach, Meshach, and Abednego get their strength?

Can you think of a time you had to stand up for something hard? Who can you turn to for strength to do hard things?

WEEK 24:
Daniel Faces the Lions' Den

SCRIPTURE REFERENCE: Daniel 6
THEME: Trust in the Lord

The Story: King Darius of Persia made Daniel an important leader. Other men who served the king didn't like Daniel. The men knew Daniel loved God. To get him in trouble, they asked the king to make a new law. It said that anyone who worshipped a god or human other than the king would go to the lions' den. Daniel prayed to God anyway, and the men told the king. Daniel was thrown into the den. He was in the den all night, but he was not touched by the lions!

God's Message: Daniel knew about the law and the consequence of praying to God instead of the king. But Daniel loved God and knew the consequences of not worshipping and praying to Him. Daniel loved the Lord more than any human or law. Could any human or law shut the lions' mouths? Only God can do that, and He did it for Daniel because he trusted the Lord.

RETELL THE STORY IN PICTURES

In the boxes below, draw what happens in the story of Daniel. Use the verses for each box to choose the part of the story you will draw!

Daniel 6:1–5

Daniel 6:6–12

Daniel 6:13–16

Daniel 6:17–28

(See page 166 for answers)

WEEK 24: DANIEL FACES THE LIONS' DEN

FOLLOW THE LEADER

Materials:

blindfold
at least 2 people

Let's experience trusting in what you can't see!

Directions: Blindfold one person. While that person (the follower) is blindfolded, the leader should set up a small obstacle course. For example, move pillows onto the floor to walk around or over. There's one important rule: NO TALKING! The leader should use these signals to guide: tap the right shoulder to turn right, tap the left shoulder to turn left, and tap between the shoulders to stop. Did you trust the leader when you were blindfolded?

Lesson: Daniel trusted God's leadership and directions so much he walked right into a lions' den! You trusted the leader to guide you while blindfolded. You can trust God so much more!

DISCUSS IT!

Is it easier to trust a friend or a stranger?

What are three things that make you trust a person?

WEEK 25:
God's Purpose for Esther

SCRIPTURE REFERENCE: Esther 2–8
THEME: You are created for a purpose

The Story: The son of King Darius, Xerxes, became the ruler of Persia after his father. King Xerxes of Persia was looking for a new queen. He chose Esther, who was a Jewish woman (the Israelites had become known as Jews). Meanwhile, Xerxes agreed to a plan to destroy the Jewish people. The king did not know Esther was a Jewish person. The new queen risked her own life by going to the king, without an invitation, to ask him to save the Jewish people. The law said anyone who went to the king without an invitation could be put to death! Her risk saved the lives of many innocent people.

God's Message: Queen Esther showed great courage and great wisdom. She asked for her people, the Jews, to pray to God and fast for her before she went to the king. She prayed and fasted, too. She did not go into the dangerous mission on her own. She leaned on God, who had created her for this purpose.

TRIVIA TIME!

Read the questions and write the answers on the lines. You can use the verses for help if you need it.

1. What did King Xerxes do after he crowned Esther? (Esther 2:17–18)

2. What secret did Esther keep from the king? (Esther 2:20)

3. Who would die if they didn't bow down to King Xerxes? (Esther 3:13)

4. What did Mordecai say to encourage Esther in the last half of verse 4:14?

5. What did Esther ask her people to do before she went to the king? (Esther 4:16)

6. What did Queen Esther say to the king when she saw him? (Esther 7:3)

(See page 166 for answers)

78 BIBLE STUDY WORKBOOK FOR KIDS

CREATED FOR A PURPOSE

Materials:

fork
measuring cup
latex balloon

Let's look at things that have been created for a purpose!

Directions: Hold the fork. What is the fork's purpose? Do the same for the measuring cup. What is its purpose? Blow up the balloon. Does it serve its purpose when it is empty or full?

Lesson: You have a purpose, too—and it is designed by God! The balloon represents us and the air inside represents God. Just like a balloon needs air to reach its full purpose, without God we miss out on the purpose He has for us.

DISCUSS IT!

What do you think God's purpose is for you? How can God use you to make a difference in the world?

Why should we follow God's instructions and trust Him in all circumstances?

WEEK 25: GOD'S PURPOSE FOR ESTHER

WEEK 26:
Nehemiah: A Man of Prayer

SCRIPTURE REFERENCE: Nehemiah 1–10
THEME: Prayer is powerful

The Story: Nehemiah was a man of prayer, and his job was to serve drinks to King Xerxes. One day, the king noticed Nehemiah was sad. Nehemiah told him he was sad because the walls of Jerusalem were broken down. With a heart of prayer, he told the king he wanted to rebuild the walls, and God answered. The king let Nehemiah leave to rebuild the walls. He even gave him supplies to get the work done!

God's Message: God worked through Nehemiah so he could rebuild the broken-down walls of Jerusalem. Nehemiah prayed to God for wisdom and strength, and God gave him those things. With God's help, Nehemiah finished the job even though his enemies tried to make his work impossible. Prayer is still powerful today. Make sure you go to God in prayer whenever you have a problem that needs solving.

AN EXAMPLE OF PRAYER

Nehemiah's prayer in Nehemiah 1:5–11 is a great example of prayer. He gives praise to God, asks for God to hear, confesses sin, speaks God's Word, shares his need, and asks for God's favor (or blessing).

Let's practice praying like Nehemiah! Use the lines below to write how your own prayer would sound.

Give God praise:

_____

Ask God to hear you:

_____

Confess a sin:

_____

Speak God's Word:

_____

Share your need:

_____

Ask for a blessing:

_____

Here are a couple of other great prayer examples in God's Word: Luke 1:46–55 and Psalm 143:1–10. Philippians 4:6 is a great verse that reminds us God wants us to go to Him with our worries in prayer!

(See page 166 for answers)

WEEK 26: NEHEMIAH: A MAN OF PRAYER

A PRAYER SANDWICH

Materials:

bread

sandwich ingredients (peanut butter, jelly, ham, tuna, etc.)

Let's see how prayers can be as different as people's favorite sandwiches!

Directions: Ask family members exactly what they want on their sandwiches. Make them. Then make your own sandwich. Finally, eat together—don't forget to pray!

Lesson: While you eat, talk about what's on your sandwiches. Is one sandwich better than the other? Nope! Just like sandwiches, there is no perfect recipe for prayer. We just need to make sure we never stop talking to God.

DISCUSS IT!

Do you ever wonder how to pray? Do you sometimes wonder if God hears your prayers?

....

....

There were a lot of verses about prayers written in this week's exercise. Which verse was your favorite?

....

....

WEEK 27:
An Unexpected King

SCRIPTURE REFERENCE: Isaiah 9:6–7, Daniel 7:13–14, 1 Timothy 6:13–15, Micah 5:2–5
THEME: Jesus was an unexpected king

The Story: Many prophets in the Old Testament told of a coming king. He would be the Son of God and would save people from their sins. Jesus had none of the qualities people expected in a king—no riches, palace, or crown. He was born in a stable and spent his time with sick and needy people. This was very different from other religious leaders who thought it was unholy to be with the sick and needy. No other king has been like Jesus! Jesus was a man, but He is also God and part of the Trinity (Jesus, God, the Holy Spirit).

God's Message: Through Jesus, God kept His promise to give us a king. The Bible is filled with kings, but none could forgive the sins of all people. Only King Jesus can save us. We really did need a different, unexpected kind of king.

THE MANY NAMES OF JESUS

Jesus is the King of kings, but He has many other names, too! Read each verse. Then look at the names in the word bank and write the name that matches on the line.

1. John 10:11 _____ _____

2. John 1:29 _____ _____ _____

3. John 1:41 _____

4. Isaiah 7:14 _____

5. Luke 2:11 _____

6. John 3:2 _____

7. John 8:12 _____ _____ _____ _____

8. Job 19:25 _____

9. Luke 19:10 _____ _____ _____

WORD BANK

Son of Man	Redeemer	Lamb of God
Good Shepherd	Immanuel	Savior
Light of the World	Messiah	Rabbi

(See page 166 for answers)

84 BIBLE STUDY WORKBOOK FOR KIDS

THAT WAS UNEXPECTED!

Materials:

clear plastic container
5 cups of warm water
raw egg
⅓ cup of salt
plastic or wooden spoon

Let's experience the unexpected!

Directions: With an adult's help, put five cups of very warm tap water into the container. Carefully place the egg in the water. What happens to the egg? Slowly add and dissolve all the salt. Stir very carefully so you don't break the egg. What does the egg do now?

Lesson: The egg in the plain water is a bit like all the kings of the earth before Jesus. They did what was expected. Jesus is like the egg that floats. When God fulfilled His promise to send a King of kings, people did not expect a king like Jesus.

DISCUSS IT!

What are some qualities of a king? Of Jesus?

What does Jesus mean to you?

WEEK 27: AN UNEXPECTED KING

WEEK 28:
Elizabeth's Very Special Visitor

SCRIPTURE REFERENCE: Luke 1:39–56
THEME: Remember to praise the Lord

The Story: Elizabeth was very old and unable to have a child, but God gave her a miracle! She became pregnant with a boy named John, who became John the Baptist. Elizabeth's cousin, Mary, was pregnant, too. When Mary visited her cousin, the Holy Spirit filled Elizabeth. The sound of Mary's voice made the baby in Elizabeth's belly jump with joy. She excitedly told Mary that both she and her child would be blessed. Mary was pregnant with Jesus! That day, both women praised the Lord.

God's Message: Imagine the joy of finding out your cousin is pregnant with the Savior! The women both knew Mary would become the mother of the one who would fulfill God's promise for a savior and king. This story reminds us to praise God for the blessings He gives each one of us.

WHAT'S THAT VERSE?

Draw a line to connect each verse to the correct part of the story.

1. Luke 1:5 — God sends the angel Gabriel to Nazareth.

2. Luke 1:13 — Mary hurried to see Elizabeth.

3. Luke 1:20 — "I bring you good news!"

4. Luke 1:26 — The generations will call Mary blessed.

5. Luke 1:39–40 — "You are to call him John."

6. Luke 1:41 — Mary stayed with Elizabeth three months.

7. Luke 1:48 — Elizabeth was Zechariah's wife.

8. Luke 1:56 — The baby leaped in Elizabeth's womb.

9. Luke 2:10 — Zechariah could not speak because he didn't believe.

Read Luke 1:46–47 and write the first part of Mary's praise below:

_____

_____

_____

_____

(See page 166 for answers)

JUMP FOR JOY!

Material:

jump rope

Let's practice praising the Lord!

Directions: Think about things that give you joy or things you are thankful for. Then get ready to jump rope. Each time you jump, sing or shout a praise for one thing that gives you joy. See how many jumps you can do. Which will you run out of first, energy or praises?

Lesson: Mary and Elizabeth had exciting news to praise God for, and you do, too. God loves you so much and has given you many things to be thankful for. In this activity, you get to exercise your body muscles *and* your praising muscles!

DISCUSS IT!

What do you do when you get exciting news? If you had great news to share, who would you tell first?

How can you praise God each day?

BIBLE STUDY WORKBOOK FOR KIDS

WEEK 29:
Jesus Is Born!

SCRIPTURE REFERENCE: Luke 1:26–38; 2:1–21, Matthew 1:18–2:15
THEME: Jesus is the perfect gift

The Story: Mary and Joseph were engaged to be married. God sent an angel named Gabriel to Mary. He told her she would be the mother of the Savior, and she should name Him Jesus! Mary became pregnant by the Holy Spirit. When it was almost time for Jesus to be born, Mary and Joseph had to travel to Bethlehem to be counted in the census. While in Bethlehem, Mary gave birth to Jesus and put Him in a manger because there was no room for them in the inns.

God's Message: Like us, Jesus was a human, but unlike us, He is also God! There were many great people in history who loved God, but none were perfect like Jesus. Since none of us do the right thing all the time, our sins break the bridge between us and God. Jesus is God's perfect gift—and the bridge back to Him. We just have to believe!

TRIVIA TIME

Read the questions and write the answers on the lines. You can use the verses for help if you need it.

1. Where did the Old Testament prophet Micah say Jesus would be born? (Micah 5:2)

2. Why did Mary and Joseph go to Bethlehem? (Luke 2:2–3)

3. Who was the king of Judea at the time? (Luke 1:5)

4. What did Gabriel tell Mary to name her son? (Luke 1:31)

5. What did the angel command Joseph to do? (Matthew 1:24)

6. What did the shepherds do when they left after seeing Jesus in the manger? (Luke 2:17)

(See pages 166–167 for answers)

THE PERFECT GIFT

Materials:

2 paper bags
crayons
candy bar
a drawing you made of baby Jesus
tissue paper

Let's see how Jesus is the best gift!

Directions: If using plain bags, decorate the bags using the crayons, making a fun gift bag. Put the candy bar in one bag and your picture of Jesus in the other. Add colorful tissue to make them pretty! Label each bag so you'll remember which is which.

Lesson: Both bags hold a gift for you. In one bag, there is a delicious treat. Open it and enjoy. Now open the other bag. The gift in the other bag represents something priceless. The gift of Jesus is yours forever, and you can give the gift of Jesus to others!

DISCUSS IT!

What is the best gift you have ever received?

Have you ever thought about Jesus as a gift that God has given to you? How can you share that gift with others?

WEEK 30:
A Message from John the Baptist

SCRIPTURE REFERENCE: Mark 1:1–8, Luke 3:1–18, Isaiah 40:3–5
THEME: Prepare your heart for Jesus

The Story: Long before John was born, God told Isaiah that a man from the wilderness would tell everyone about the Savior of the world. John lived in the wilderness, wore clothes made from camel hair, and ate bugs! He was the man from Isaiah's prophecy. John the Baptist helped make the way for Jesus. He told people to repent, which means to turn from sin. Some thought he might be the Messiah. John baptized people with water, but he told everyone that the one after him would baptize with the Holy Spirit.

God's Message: The prophets of the Old Testament preached that a savior and king was coming. John the Baptist introduced the world to this king, Jesus. Today, you can tell the world about the Savior. The difference is, the prophets and John were telling of a savior who was coming, but you get to tell the good news that Jesus, our Savior, is here!

ANNOUNCE THE GOOD NEWS!

Look up the words below in a physical or online dictionary. Using what you learned and your creativity, draw a picture or write down the definition in the box.

Baptism

Messiah

Repent

Prophecy

(See page 167 for answers)

WEEK 30: A MESSAGE FROM JOHN THE BAPTIST

ANNOUNCING THE NEWS OF THE SAVIOR

Materials:

marker
index cards or strips of paper
Bible

Let's use John's words to make a path to Jesus!

Directions: Look up each of the things John the Baptist said in these verses: Matthew 3:2; Luke 3:11, 3:14; and Mark 1:3, 1:7, 1:8. Write each sentence on an index card or strip of paper. Make a path on the floor with the cards. Now walk the path of John's word!

Lesson: John the Baptist said things like "Repent," "Share your clothes," "After me, One is coming who is mightier!" People thought John might be the Messiah, but he made it clear the real Savior was coming. His words were like a path leading people to Jesus.

DISCUSS IT!

John taught that the way to prepare our hearts is to repent of our sin. What does it mean to repent?

How can you prepare your own heart for Jesus?

WEEK 31: Temptation in the Wilderness

SCRIPTURE REFERENCE: Matthew 4:1–11
THEME: God's Word is our guide

The Story: After Jesus was baptized, He wandered through the wilderness for 40 days and 40 nights. Jesus didn't eat the whole time. By the end, the devil thought he could tempt Him because He was weak with hunger. He tested Jesus three different times. Once he even told Jesus he would give Him all the kingdoms on Earth if Jesus would bow to him. Every single time, Jesus answered the devil with the truth of God's Word.

God's Message: The devil used God's Word to tempt Jesus, but Jesus knew God's Word better. He used scripture to resist the devil's twisted lies. Like Jesus, we need to know God's Word because the devil tempts us, too—and he is just as sneaky. We can be tempted to sin, but knowing God's Word helps us make godly choices. God's Word should be the guide we use for our lives.

JESUS IN THE WILDERNESS

Use this page to draw a picture of Jesus in the wilderness. What did he wear? Were there any animals around? Maybe even add the devil. What does he look like? Draw a quote bubble over Jesus. Inside, write one of the verses from Luke 4:1–12 that Jesus spoke to resist the devil.

(See page 167 for answers)

96 BIBLE STUDY WORKBOOK FOR KIDS

RESIST TEMPTATION

Materials:

an adult
M&M's or small marshmallows
timer

Let's see how tough it can be to be tempted.

Directions: Have an adult give you one M&M or marshmallow, but don't eat it yet. Set the timer for 30 minutes. If you can wait to eat the one treat in front of you until the timer ends, you will get ten more! You can do something else while you wait.

Lesson: Sometimes it's hard for us to wait, but when we know God and His Word, we trust He always has better things in store for us.

DISCUSS IT!

How did Jesus resist the devil's temptations?

Do you have any scripture memorized? What did you learn about the importance of knowing God's Word?

WEEK 32:
Jesus Calls the Twelve Disciples

SCRIPTURE REFERENCE: Matthew 4:18–22; 28:16–20, Mark 3:13–19
THEME: Jesus wants us to follow Him

The Story: Twelve of Jesus's closest followers were called His disciples. Some were fishermen who left their boats and nets by the water. One was a tax man who left a job that made him good money. These men sacrificed everything to follow Jesus. Jesus called them to teach others, perform miracles, and make even more disciples!

God's Message: It is a lot to ask a person to drop everything and follow someone they don't know, but Jesus isn't just anyone. He is God! There was something special that convinced the disciples to follow Him. Jesus now wants all of us to be His disciples. God has called all believers to tell the world about His love and salvation. That means you, too. You are called to tell people about the good news of Jesus!

TEST YOURSELF!

Write the letter of each disciple's matching description on the line. You can check the verses if you get stuck. One letter will be used twice!

1. ___ Simon Peter
2. ___ Andrew
3. ___ James
4. ___ Philip
5. ___ Nathanael
6. ___ Matthew
7. ___ Thomas
8. ___ John
9. ___ James
10. ___ Simon
11. ___ Judas Iscariot
12. ___ Judas/Jude/Thaddeus

A. a tax collector (Matthew 9:9)

B. betrayed Jesus (Matthew 10:4)

C. told Peter, "We have found the Messiah" (John 1:40–42)

D. called by Jesus when fishing on a boat (Mark 1:19–20)

E. from Bethsaida (John 1:44)

F. needed to see the nail marks in Jesus's hands to believe He'd risen (John 20:24–25)

G. was called the Zealot (Luke 6:15)

H. was called several names. One name was the same as another disciple, but this one did not betray Jesus. (John 14:22)

I. asked Jesus, "How do you know me?" (John 1:48)

J. denied Jesus three times (Matthew 26:69–75)

K. son of Alphaeus (Matthew 10:3)

(See page 167 for answers)

CHANGE THE WORLD

Materials:

food coloring
clear glass filled with water
spoon

Let's see how telling people about Jesus can affect the world.

Directions: Put one drop of food coloring into the glass of water. Using the spoon, stir the water and watch as the color of all the water changes.

Lesson: The water in the glass represents the world and the food coloring is the good news about Jesus. The spoon represents you with God's call for you to share Jesus with others. See what happens when you obey God's call?

DISCUSS IT!

What made Jesus so special that the disciples left everything to follow Him?

_____

_____

What are some ways you can share Jesus in your home, school, or city?

_____

_____

WEEK 33:
Feeding Five Thousand!

SCRIPTURE REFERENCE: John 6:1–14
THEME: God always provides

The Story: One day, Jesus was healing the sick and preaching to more than 5,000 people on the shore of a lake. It was late and there was no food to feed everyone. Andrew found a boy who had five loaves of bread and two fish. The boy offered them to Jesus. Jesus took the food and gave thanks to God for it. Then He turned it into enough food to feed the whole crowd. When all the people finished eating, there were twelve baskets of food left over!

God's Message: God used the generous boy's food to provide for a large group of people. No matter how little, Jesus can and will use whatever we have for His good. Everything you offer to Jesus is valuable to Him. In this story, we see that when we seek Jesus, God provides for our needs and more!

QUICK QUIZ

Circle the correct answer to each question in the quiz.

1. People followed Jesus to hear Him preach and see Him _____.

   a. make furniture
   b. heal the sick
   c. dance

2. How many people were in the crowd?

   a. 5,000
   b. 500
   c. 1,000

3. How much food did the boy have?

   a. five loaves, two fish
   b. two loaves, five fish
   c. three loaves, one fish

4. Before Jesus passed out the food, He _____.

   a. gave thanks
   b. had a taste
   c. sniffed it

5. How many extra baskets of food did the disciples pick up?

   a. 5,000
   b. five
   c. twelve

If this miracle was a headline on the news, what would the headline say?

_____

(See page 167 for answers)

BIBLE STUDY WORKBOOK FOR KIDS

MORE TO GIVE

Materials:

piece of paper
scissors

Let's make more to provide for others.

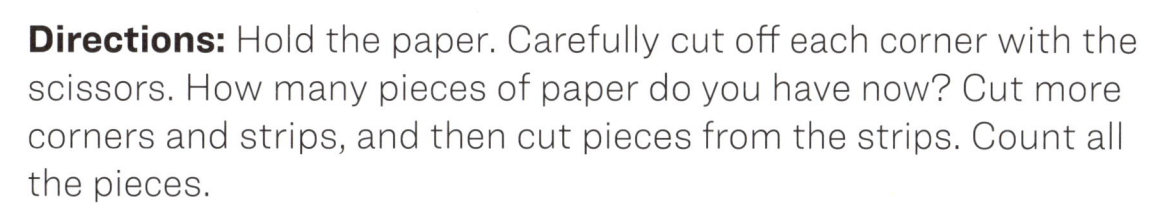

Directions: Hold the paper. Carefully cut off each corner with the scissors. How many pieces of paper do you have now? Cut more corners and strips, and then cut pieces from the strips. Count all the pieces.

Lesson: You have a lot of pieces of paper you can share now. The more Jesus divided the loaves and fishes, the more He had to give, and it was more than enough! Jesus used a boy's lunch to bless thousands, and He can do the same using what you have, too.

DISCUSS IT!

What are some things you can share with others?

The disciples worried there would be no food to feed the people. What do you worry about? Can you trust God for those things?

WEEK 33: FEEDING FIVE THOUSAND!

WEEK 34:
Jesus Calms the Storm

SCRIPTURE REFERENCE: Mark 4:35–41, Matthew 6:25–34
THEME: Trust God to protect you

The Story: Jesus and His disciples were on a boat on the Sea of Galilee. Suddenly, a strong storm came while Jesus was sleeping. Some of the disciples had been fishermen, so they knew how dangerous storms could be. They woke Jesus because they were afraid. Jesus told the wind and waves to be still, and they calmed. Jesus asked, "Why are you so afraid?" He was surprised the disciples didn't trust Him to take care of them after all the miracles they had seen Him do.

God's Message: Sometimes we let worry take over and forget to have faith in Jesus. When you have a hard time trusting God, remember how surprised Jesus was when the disciples didn't show faith by trusting in Him. Just as with the disciples in that boat, Jesus expects and wants us to trust in Him, too!

WHAT WAS IT LIKE?

Read Mark 4:35–41. Imagine you are a disciple on the boat with Jesus during the storm. Draw a picture to show what it was like!

(See page 167 for answers)

WEEK 34: JESUS CALMS THE STORM

FAITH IN A CHAIR

Material:

chair

Let's use a chair to help us understand faith in Jesus.

Directions: Choose a chair to sit on and stand in front of it. Now turn around, and with your back to the chair, sit in the chair.

Lesson: Why did you choose the chair you did? You probably picked a chair you trusted. You had faith that your chair would do what it was made to do! We can count on Jesus to do what He said He will do. Like the disciples, we might forget to trust Him, so each time you sit in a chair, remember your faith in Jesus!

DISCUSS IT!

How would you have felt if you were a disciple on the boat?

_____

_____

It can be hard to have faith in things you can't see. What are some things you have faith in that you can't see (for example, we can't see wind and sound, but we know they're there)?

_____

_____

WEEK 35:
Nicodemus: A Curious Pharisee

SCRIPTURE REFERENCE: John 3:1–17
THEME: You must be born again

The Story: Pharisees were not allowed to talk to Jesus because of their beliefs. There was a Pharisee named Nicodemus who wanted to talk to Jesus. They met at night to talk so Nicodemus would not get in trouble. He believed Jesus was the Son of God. Jesus told Nicodemus that in order to enter God's kingdom, he must be born again, but not as a baby—in the Spirit!

God's Message: When Jesus told Nicodemus he had to be born again, He wasn't talking about a new body, but the Holy Spirit. Our new birth happens when we believe in and follow Jesus. When Jesus was baptized by John the Baptist, the Holy Spirit was present. God gives us the Holy Spirit, too! When we trust in Jesus, we can have God's spirit in us, and through faith we are born again.

FILL IN THE BLANKS

Pick the correct word from the word bank to complete each sentence. You can check the verses if you get stuck.

1. The Pharisee named _____ came to see Jesus. (John 3:1)

2. Nicodemus visited Jesus secretly at _____ because Pharisees were not allowed to speak to Jesus. (John 3:2)

3. Nicodemus believed Jesus was from God because of the _____ He was doing. (John 3:2)

4. Jesus told him a person must be _____ again to enter the kingdom of God. (John 3:3)

5. Nicodemus thought by being "born again," Jesus meant becoming a _____ again. (John 3:4)

6. What did Jesus compare the Holy Spirit to? _____ (John 3:8)

WORD BANK

| baby | wind | miracles |
| Nicodemus | born | night |

(See page 167 for answers)

A LITTLE WIND

Materials:

2 balloons
2 people

Let's see how air is like the Holy Spirit.

Directions: Each person should blow up their balloon while the other watches. Be sure to tie the balloons when they are full.

Lesson: When you blow up a balloon, you are blowing air inside it. Do you see the air blowing in? Now look at the balloons. Can you see the air inside them? Just like the Holy Spirit, you can't see the air blowing into the balloons or the air inside, but you know it's there. That's like our faith in the Holy Spirit and the new birth Jesus told Nicodemus about.

DISCUSS IT!

Had you heard the words "born again" before? What do those words mean to you?

What are ways the Holy Spirit speaks to us?

WEEK 36:
Jesus: The Great Healer

SCRIPTURE REFERENCE: Mark 2:1–12, Matthew 8:1–4, Luke 7:1–10; 8:43–48
THEME: Jesus heals

The Story: During His time on Earth, Jesus healed a lot of people! He healed people who couldn't walk, or were blind or deaf. He healed others with leprosy, a terrible skin disease. Jesus once healed an officer's servant without even going to his house. One woman had so much faith in Jesus that she was healed by simply touching His robe. A man even had his friends lower him through a roof down to Jesus to be healed!

God's Message: No wonder people followed Jesus around everywhere! Jesus showed love, acceptance, and compassion to all people. He wasn't afraid to be with sick people and even touched people with leprosy. Jesus was never far away from those who needed Him, and He is still with us! We can always turn to Him to help us when we are sick or in pain.

WHAT'S THAT VERSE?

Write the letter of the verse that matches the person Jesus healed.

1. ___ a man who was lowered through the roof
2. ___ a man who had leprosy
3. ___ a servant of an officer who was about to die
4. ___ a blind man

A. Luke 7:1–10

B. John 9:1–12

C. Matthew 8:2–3

D. Mark 2:3–5

Which story is your favorite? In the box below, either draw or write about it in your own words!

(See page 167 for answers)

WEEK 36: JESUS: THE GREAT HEALER

MAKE IT WHOLE

Materials:

piece of white paper
crayons
scissors
tape

Let's see an example of Jesus taking on our sin and disease.

Directions: Draw a picture on the paper of one of the healing stories you read about in this week's lesson. Cut the picture into six to eight pieces. Then tape it back together!

Lesson: In this example, your artwork represents you and the tape represents Jesus. When you are feeling broken or hurt, Jesus can heal you and make you whole again! When you have faith in Jesus, He is never far away.

DISCUSS IT!

Why do you think Jesus healed people?

....

....

How do you think you would react if you saw a healing miracle?

....

....

....

WEEK 37:
Mary, Martha, and Jesus

SCRIPTURE REFERENCE: Luke 10:38–42
THEME: Put Jesus first

The Story: Jesus and His disciples were in a town and a woman named Martha invited them to her house. Martha did a lot of work for her guests while her sister Mary sat at Jesus's feet listening to Him. Martha was annoyed that Mary wasn't helping her. She spoke to Jesus about it. Jesus lovingly told her that she worries about so many things, but only one thing is important. He explained that putting Him first is more important than what she was worrying about.

God's Message: Someday, your life will be very busy. When things take your attention away from Jesus, it's good to remember this story. Jesus loved both women so much—the busy one and the one who sat at His feet—and Jesus loves you, too! He loves you no matter what, but His heart wants you to come to Him.

USE YOUR TIME WISELY

Think about your daily chores and some ways you can spend time with Jesus. Write or draw your ideas in the following boxes.

Three ways to spend time with Jesus

Three chores I need to do

[empty box]

What can you do to make sure you are able to come to Jesus every day?

_____

_____

_____

_____

(See page 167 for answers)

WEEK 37: MARY, MARTHA, AND JESUS

MAKE ROOM TO COME TO JESUS

Materials:

3 Ping-Pong balls or small rocks
container with a lid
dry rice
bowl

Let's see how easy it is to make room for Jesus when you put Him first.

Directions: Put the balls in the container and then fill the container the rest of the way with rice. Put on the lid. Now remove the lid and pour everything in the bowl. Remove the balls. Pour just the rice into the container. Can you fit the balls into the container now?

Lesson: The balls represent Jesus, God's Word, and prayer. The rice represents everything else in our lives. When we put Jesus first, there is always room in our lives to come to Him!

DISCUSS IT!

How would you have felt if you were Martha?

Why do you think Jesus said Mary's choice was more important? How does that affect your choices?

WEEK 38:
A Good Neighbor

SCRIPTURE REFERENCE: Luke 10:25–37, Matthew 22:37–39
THEME: Love and care for everyone

The Story: A lawyer knew he needed to love the Lord and his neighbors, but he had a question for Jesus. He asked, "Who is my neighbor?" Jesus answered with a parable. A Jewish man had been attacked and was left wounded on the side of the road. A priest and a Levite both saw the man and passed by without helping. When a Samaritan saw the man, he cared for his wounds, and put the man on his donkey. He took him to an inn to take care of him. He even paid for everything! Jews and Samaritans didn't treat each other kindly back then, but the Samaritan took care of the man anyway.

God's Message: In this story, Jesus teaches us that everyone is our neighbor—not just our friends or those who live next door. It is easy to care for people you know and love, but God has called us to love and care for everyone.

TRUE OR FALSE?

Read Luke 10:25–37. Then circle the correct answer to each question.

1. Jesus told this story because a man asked Him, "Who is my neighbor?"

   True   False

2. The man was hurt because he tripped and fell.

   True   False

3. The priest helped the wounded man.

   True   False

4. A Levite saw the man and went to the other side of the road.

   True   False

5. The Samaritan put bandages on the man's wounds while still on the road.

   True   False

6. The Samaritan paid for the Jewish man's stay at the inn.

   True   False

7. This parable teaches us how important it is to show love to everyone.

   True   False

8. Only people we know are our neighbors.

   True   False

(See page 167 for answers)

LOVING OTHERS CAN BE DIRTY WORK

Materials:

small plant or wildflower with roots
empty pot (to replant the plant)
soil

Let's roll up our sleeves and see how loving our neighbors sometimes means getting a little dirty.

Directions: With your parent or guardian, find a plant or wildflower in your yard, at the store, or from a neighbor or community garden. No gloves allowed! Use your hands to replant the plant or wildflower in the new pot. Be sure the roots are attached when replanting and add soil as needed.

Lesson: Helping someone might be messy, but it is what Jesus calls us to do. We are to love everyone.

DISCUSS IT!

Is there someone in your life who is hard to love? Why do you need to love them anyway?

_____

_____

What would you have done if you were the Samaritan?

_____

_____

WEEK 38: A GOOD NEIGHBOR

WEEK 39:
The Lost Son

SCRIPTURE REFERENCE: Luke 15:10–24
THEME: We can always return to God

The Story: In this parable, Jesus talks about a son who asked his father for his share of the inheritance to go live how he wanted. Over time, he wasted all the money and had to get a job feeding pigs. He was so poor and hungry he was willing to eat the pigs' food! Then he remembered that his father's servants lived better than he was living. He went back home to ask to be a servant. When his father saw him coming from far down the road, he ran to his son, hugged him, and threw a big party because his son returned!

God's Message: The father in this story represents God, and the son represents all of us. God loves us so much that when we sin, He does not kick us out of His family. Instead, His heart is full of joy when we repent and come back to Him. He opens His arms wide for us and celebrates!

WHAT DOES IT MEAN?

Draw a line to match each word with its meaning. It's okay to use a dictionary if you need help.

1. prodigal — to be sorry for sins
2. inheritance — kindness from someone with power
3. mercy — a story that teaches a lesson
4. repent — wasteful, spends too much
5. parable — money and property you get when a person dies

Draw your favorite scene from the story.

(See page 168 for answers)

WEEK 39: THE LOST SON

PARTY INVITATION

Materials:

white construction paper
markers or paint and paintbrushes
stickers and glitter (optional)

Let's celebrate the son's return and make a party invitation!

Directions: The father was so happy to have his son back! What do you think the father would have included on his invitation? Make an invitation to the party that the father threw for his son.

Lesson: In Luke 15:10, it says that even the angels rejoice when a sinner turns away from sin. It's almost like a party in heaven! Remember that nothing makes God happier than to have His children come back to Him. His invitation is always out there for you to return home.

DISCUSS IT!

When you do something wrong, what do you expect will happen? What do you hope will happen?

What can you expect from God when you repent?

WEEK 40:
Lazarus, Come Out!

SCRIPTURE REFERENCE: John 11
THEME: God's timing is perfect

The Story: Martha and Mary's brother, Lazarus, was sick. Jesus knew this, but He waited to go to him. Jesus knew that whatever happened, Lazarus would be healed. By the time Jesus arrived, Lazarus had been dead for four days and was already buried. The sisters told Jesus if He had come earlier, their brother would not have died. Jesus went to Lazarus's tomb and said, "Lazarus, come out!" As everyone watched, Lazarus walked out, alive and healthy!

God's Message: This miracle shows that Jesus is life, and those who believe in Him can have life forever with Him! Mary and Martha didn't understand at first why Jesus didn't come sooner. It can be hard for us to understand God's timing, too. Sometimes we don't know why we must wait, but we can always trust that God's timing will be the very best for us.

FILL IN THE BLANKS

Jesus raised two other people from the dead! Read Luke 7:11–16 and Luke 8:41–56. Pick the correct word from the word bank to complete each sentence. You can check the verses if you get stuck.

1. Jesus went to a town called _____. (Luke 7:11)

2. He met a woman whose son was _____. (Luke 7:12)

3. Jesus felt sad for the woman and told her not to _____. (Luke 7:13)

4. He went up and touched the dead man and told him to _____. (Luke 7:14)

5. Those who saw, _____ God. (Luke 7:16)

6. Jairus's daughter was _____ years old and dying. (Luke 8:42)

7. A _____ from Jairus's house came to say his daughter was dead. (Luke 8:49)

8. Jesus heard the messenger and said not to fear. He said she was _____ and not dead. (Luke 8:52)

WORD BANK

dead	get up	asleep
messenger	twelve	praised
cry	Nain	

(See page 168 for answers)

TRUST IN WAITING

Materials:

3 to 5 dried beans
small, clear plastic cup
paper towel

Let's practice waiting for the right time.

Directions: Soak the beans in water overnight. Dampen the paper towel and place it in the bottom of the cup, pressing it against the sides. Tuck the beans into the damp paper towel. Place the cup in a sunny spot. Add a little water when the paper towel dries out. You should see sprouts in a few days.

Lesson: The beans you planted will sprout, but not right away. Trusting God and His timing can be a bit like waiting for beans to sprout. You don't know exactly when, but it will happen.

DISCUSS IT!

Can you think of a time when you had to wait when you didn't understand why?

Why do you think Jesus made Mary and Martha wait?

WEEK 40: LAZARUS, COME OUT!

WEEK 41:
Jesus Teaches Us How to Pray

SCRIPTURE REFERENCE: Matthew 6:5–13
THEME: Prayer is talking to God

The Story: Jesus prayed a lot! He often spent time by Himself praying to God, His Father. One day, one of the disciples asked Jesus to teach them to pray. In Matthew 6:9–13, Jesus gave a very specific prayer that most people know as the Lord's Prayer.

God's Message: The Lord's Prayer teaches us how to pray. In the prayer, Jesus shows us three things that we should include when talking to God in prayer: praising and thanking Him, asking for forgiveness, and then asking for things and help. God does want us to ask Him for things, but He doesn't want that to be all we do when we pray! Prayer helps us get to know God and brings us closer to Him. Jesus set a great example by showing us how important prayer was for Him every day.

WEEK 42:
Zacchaeus Finds Jesus

SCRIPTURE REFERENCE: Luke 19:1–10
THEME: Those who seek God find Him

The Story: Jesus went to Jericho, where a rich tax collector named Zacchaeus lived. This man was curious about Jesus, but he was short and couldn't see Him over the crowd. He climbed a tree for a better view. Jesus saw Zacchaeus and called to the man to come out of the tree. Then Jesus said He was going to stay at Zacchaeus's house. People were surprised because tax collectors were thought to be cheaters and thieves. After speaking with Jesus, Zacchaeus's heart was changed. He told Jesus he'd give half his things to the poor and would pay back four times the amount of money he had stolen.

God's Message: Zacchaeus's curiosity about Jesus changed his life forever. Today, we find Jesus through other ways, like prayer and studying God's Word. God promises in His Word that if we seek Him, we will find Him.

ALL ABOUT ZACCHAEUS

Read Luke 19:1–10. Draw the trunk and branches of the tree Zacchaeus climbed. On the leaves of the tree, write six facts from the story that stand out to you. Beneath the tree, draw Jesus and Zacchaeus after Jesus called him down from the tree.

(See page 168 for answers)

130 BIBLE STUDY WORKBOOK FOR KIDS

SEEK AND FIND

Material:

a friend, sibling, or family member

Let's play hide-and-seek!

Directions: Close your eyes and count to ten while your partner finds a good hiding place, and then start seeking! Next, have them hide in a place that is a little obvious. Was it easier to find them?

Lesson: Jeremiah 29:13 tells us that when we seek God, we will find Him. When you play this game, remember there is one big difference when it comes to you seeking God. God never hides from us! If you look for Him, you will find Him. It's a promise from God!

DISCUSS IT!

What does it mean to seek? Is God hard to find?

How can you seek God each day?

WEEK 42: ZACCHAEUS FINDS JESUS

WEEK 43:
Jesus: The King

SCRIPTURE REFERENCE: Luke 19:28–40
THEME: Jesus is the King of kings

The Story: Jesus and His disciples came to Jerusalem. When they were close, Jesus sent two disciples into town to bring back a specific donkey. The disciples laid their coats on the donkey for Jesus to sit on. Then Jesus rode the donkey into Jerusalem while crowds of people laid down their coats for the donkey to walk on. They praised their new king, shouting "Hosanna!" The Pharisees told Jesus to make them be quiet, but nothing could stop the joy of the people.

God's Message: The prophets of the Old Testament told of a king to come. When Jesus rode into Jerusalem, many thought He was the king they had been waiting for, and He was, but He was a different kind of king. Jesus did not come to wear a crown, lead armies, or rule with law. He came to save us from our sin, lead with love, and rule over our hearts. Jesus is the King of kings!

WHAT'S THAT VERSE?

Many Old Testament prophets told of a coming king. Do you remember learning about prophets in Week 22? Write the letter of the verse that matches each prophecy about Jesus.

1. ___ He would be born of a woman.　　　　A. Zechariah 9:9

2. ___ He would be born in Bethlehem.　　　B. Psalm 78:1–2

3. ___ A messenger would prepare the way.　C. Isaiah 53:3

4. ___ He could come as a king on a donkey.　D. Daniel 7:14

5. ___ He would speak in parables or stories.　E. Micah 5:2

6. ___ He would heal people.　　　　　　　　F. Isaiah 35:5–6

7. ___ He would be hated and rejected.　　　G. Isaiah 7:14

8. ___ His kingdom would never be destroyed.　H. Isaiah 40:3–5

(See page 168 for answers)

WEEK 43: JESUS: THE KING

SEE THE BIGGER PICTURE

Materials:

paper towel tube
handful of small items like M&M's or dried beans
small cup or bowl

Let's see what it's like not being able to see the big picture.

Directions: Spread the items on a table. Look through the tube with one eye and close the other. With your free hand, pick up all the M&M's you see through the tube and put them in the cup. Spread the M&M's out on the table again. This time, don't use the tube to find the M&M's.

Lesson: Looking through the tube represents those in Jerusalem who thought Jesus was going to be a regular king. They just didn't see the bigger picture!

DISCUSS IT!

What does a regular king look like? What would a parade for a regular king look like?

How would you describe Jesus to if someone asked?

WEEK 44:
The Last Supper

SCRIPTURE REFERENCE: Luke 22:7–24
THEME: The first communion

The Story: While the Jews were enslaved in Egypt, God sent a plague to kill all the firstborn sons in Egypt. He passed over the houses of Jewish firstborn boys and spared their lives. This became known as Passover. Jesus and the disciples met to celebrate Passover. Jesus washed the disciples' feet. He also said one of them, Judas, would betray Him that night. Then Jesus broke the bread, gave it to the disciples, and called it His body. After, He passed them a cup of wine and called it His blood. He told them His blood would be given to forgive the sins of all. This was the first communion.

God's Message: The disciples did not understand Jesus's words about His body and His blood at the time. We now know that Jesus was talking about His death and resurrection. When we take communion today, we are remembering the Last Supper. We also remember the sacrifice Jesus made so that the world could be saved.

RETELL THE STORY

Read Luke 22:7–38 and put the events in order by numbering them from 1 to 4. You can use the verse references for help.

____ Jesus showed who would betray Him. (Luke 22:21)

____ Jesus broke bread and shared the cup with His disciples. (Luke 22:19)

____ The disciples argued about which of them is the greatest. (Luke 22:24)

____ Jesus sent two disciples to prepare for the Passover meal. (Luke 22:8)

Read Exodus 12. What foods do you think everyone ate at the Last Supper?

....

....

....

What would you have said or done if Jesus wanted to wash your feet?

....

....

....

(See page 168 for answers)

136 BIBLE STUDY WORKBOOK FOR KIDS

PLAN TO SHARE A MEAL

Materials:

food
table and chairs
your family

Let's make and share a meal with your family.

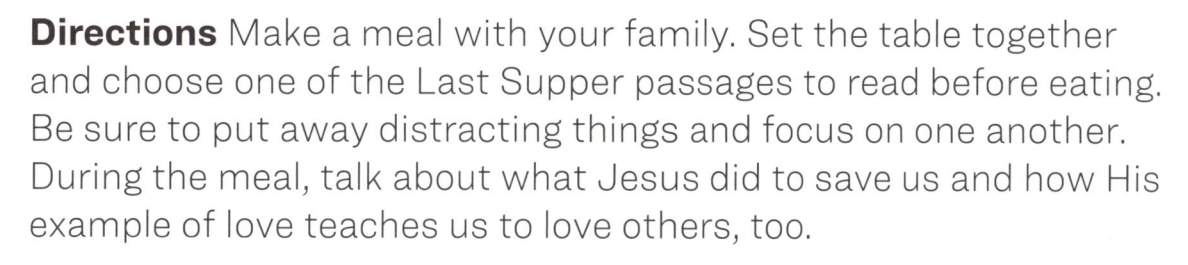

Directions Make a meal with your family. Set the table together and choose one of the Last Supper passages to read before eating. Be sure to put away distracting things and focus on one another. During the meal, talk about what Jesus did to save us and how His example of love teaches us to love others, too.

Lesson: Just like Jesus spent the Last Supper teaching and sharing His love with His disciples, it's important to spend time learning about Jesus together and showing His love to one another.

DISCUSS IT!

Why are Old Testament stories, like the story of Passover, important to us today?

How would you have felt if you were at the table with Jesus?

WEEK 44: THE LAST SUPPER

WEEK 45:
Jesus in Gethsemane

SCRIPTURE REFERENCE: Matthew 26:36–55
THEME: Prayer gives comfort and strength

The Story: After the Last Supper, Jesus and the disciples went to the Garden of Gethsemane. All the disciples came along, but Jesus took Peter, James, and John with Him into the garden and asked them to keep watch while He went to pray. Jesus asked His Father if there was a way to spare His life but told God He would do His will. When Jesus was finished, Judas came and betrayed Jesus. Guards with swords and clubs took Jesus away.

God's Message: Jesus knew His prayer would not change what He had to do. He also knew where His comfort and strength would come from—God, His Father. Jesus set an important example for us through His prayer time in the garden. God is our Father, too. Like He did for Jesus, He will strengthen us when we go to Him.

FILL IN THE BLANKS

Pick the correct word from the word bank to complete each sentence. You can check the verses if you get stuck.

1. Jesus prayed in _____. (Mark 14:32)

2. Jesus asked Peter, _____, and John to stand guard for him. (Mark 14:33)

3. Judas betrayed Jesus with a _____. (Luke 22:48)

4. Jesus said, "Yet not my will, but _____ be done." (Luke 22:42)

5. When Jesus returned to Peter, James, and John, they were _____. (Mark 14:37)

6. Peter used a _____ to cut off a soldier's ear. (John 18:10)

7. An _____ appeared and strengthened Jesus. (Luke 22:43)

8. Jesus's sweat was like drops of _____. (Luke 22:44)

9. The soldiers brought Jesus to a man named _____ after he was arrested. (John 18:13–14)

WORD BANK

Annas	sword	kiss
sleeping	James	Yours
blood	angel	Gethsemane

(See page 168 for answers)

WEEK 45: JESUS IN GETHSEMANE

THE WEIGHT IS LIFTED!

Materials:

4 to 6 heavy books
a partner

Let's see how prayer can help it feel like a weight is being lifted from us.

Directions: Hold the books and share things that make you feel worried, scared, or hurt. Each time you share a concern, your partner should take a book from your stack. The burden is lighter each time!

Lesson: When we share our feelings, needs, and heart with God, it is a lot like letting go of those heavy books. Just like the angel strengthened Jesus when He prayed, God comforts and strengthens you when you ask for His help during difficult times.

DISCUSS IT!

What are some things that you can talk to God about?

....

....

When you are scared or upset, how do you usually behave? What do you think Jesus would tell you to do?

....

....

WEEK 46:
Jesus Died and Lives Again!

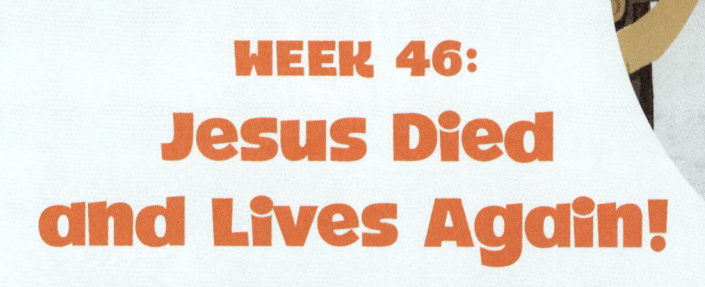

SCRIPTURE REFERENCE: Matthew 27:11–28:20
THEME: Jesus saved us from sin

The Story: After Jesus was taken from the garden, He was put on trial and sentenced to death on a cross. Jesus was beaten, made fun of, and forced to wear a crown of thorns. He also had to carry His own cross. Even in His pain, He prayed for the people who hurt Him. Three days after Jesus died, women went to the tomb to prepare His body for burial, but they found the tomb empty. Jesus had risen from the dead!

God's Message: The crowd that cheered for Jesus to be killed did not know that God had a plan for His purpose and our good. Jesus rose from the grave after three days to finish the work He came to do. His suffering, death, and resurrection ended the separation between us and God. Jesus went through all that pain so you, me, everyone you love, and every person on Earth would have the freedom to choose to live forever with Him!

HAPPY EASTER!

Easter is the day we celebrate Jesus's resurrection and the amazing sacrifice He made for us. What does Easter mean to you? Draw a picture of Jesus after He was raised from the dead and write the first sentence of Matthew 28:6 below your picture.

(See page 169 for answers)

JESUS TOOK ON OUR SIN AT THE CROSS

Materials:

votive candle and a match
small glass plate
colored water
tall, clear drinking glass
an adult

Let's see an example of Jesus taking up our sin.

Directions: Put the candle in the middle of the plate and pour a little water around its base so the bottom of the plate is just covered. Ask an adult to light the candle and let it burn for a minute. Then ask the adult to put the glass, upside down, over the candle to create a seal with the water. Watch what happens.

Lesson: The candle represents Jesus, the glass represents the cross, and the water represents our sin. When Jesus died for us on the cross, He took on our sin.

DISCUSS IT!

Why was it important for Jesus to rise from the dead?

Imagine you were one of the women who went to the tomb. What do you think you would have thought and felt?

WEEK 46: JESUS DIED AND LIVES AGAIN!

WEEK 47:
Saul Sees the Light

SCRIPTURE REFERENCE: Acts 9:1–31; 13:9
THEME: We can all be changed by Jesus

The Story: Saul, later known as the Apostle Paul, was a Jewish man who hated those who followed Jesus. He had many followers put into prison and killed for sharing the message of Jesus. One day, while on the road to Damascus, Saul saw a bright light. He fell to the ground and heard a voice say, "Why do you persecute me?" That voice was Jesus! Saul was blinded by the light, but God sent a man named Ananias to heal Saul's sight.

God's Message: After Saul got his sight back, he changed. He stopped putting Christians in jail and began to share the gospel of Jesus. When we turn from our sin and believe in Jesus, our lives and hearts are changed forever!

PAUL IS CHANGED BY GOD

Read Acts 9:1–31. In each small box, write a fact about Saul. In the big box, draw a picture of Saul when the light from heaven came upon him.

Write the words of 2 Corinthians 5:17 on the line below!

(See page 169 for answers)

WEEK 47: SAUL SEES THE LIGHT

A CHANGE OF HEART

Materials:

an egg
container with a lid
vinegar

Let's change an egg to represent the change in Saul's heart.

Directions: Put the egg into the container. Fill the container with vinegar, making sure to cover the egg. Put on the lid and let the egg sit for three days. Remove the egg. How has it changed?

Lesson: The egg represents Saul's hard heart, and the vinegar represents Jesus. The vinegar turned the egg's hard shell into something soft and rubbery. When Jesus comes into our hearts, we are completely changed—just like the egg!

DISCUSS IT!

Can anyone change or just some people? Explain your answer.

Does Jesus only care about people who believe in Him? Why or why not?

WEEK 48:
A Miracle through Tabitha and Peter

SCRIPTURE REFERENCE: Acts 9:36–43
THEME: Jesus works through us

The Story: Tabitha (also called Dorcas) was a disciple who always did good things. She helped the poor by making clothing for them. After Tabitha died, Peter came to her home. Women were mourning, and they showed him the many clothes Tabitha had made. He went to the room where she was, got on his knees, and prayed. Then he told her to wake up, and she did! This miracle helped many people believe in Jesus.

God's Message: Jesus works through us when we help others. Tabitha's hard work for people who needed help was a way Jesus worked through her. Jesus worked through Peter to raise Tabitha from the dead! When we let Jesus work through us, amazing things can happen. Tabitha and Peter are great examples of Jesus working through people. Jesus can work through you, too!

TRUE OR FALSE?

Read Acts 9:36–43. Then circle the correct answer to each question.

1. Tabitha was also known as Dorcas.

   True   False

2. Tabitha was known for cooking food.

   True   False

3. Peter was in Lydda, a nearby town, when two men came for him.

   True   False

4. Before going to see Tabitha, Peter ate a snack.

   True   False

5. Tabitha was only sleeping.

   True   False

6. Many new people believed in the Lord because Tabitha was raised from the dead.

   True   False

Jesus works through us when we help others. On the lines below, write ideas for how you can help others (for example: help your parents make dinner or help your brother with his homework).

_____

_____

_____

(See page 169 for answers)

DIFFERENT TOOLS

Materials:

several different tools (for example, a hammer, screwdriver, ruler, whisk, spoon)
pencil
piece of paper

Let's discover how different tools do different things.

Directions: Pick up each tool and write down what each one can be used for.

Lesson: Just like each tool is different and is useful for a different job than the other tools, each of us is different. Jesus can work through every person, and He uses us all in different ways to do different things. His purpose is always the same—to glorify Him through us.

DISCUSS IT!

Raising someone from the dead is pretty cool, but there are many other ways Jesus works through people. What is a way Jesus can work through you?

_____

_____

How does it make you feel when someone helps you?

_____

_____

WEEK 48: A MIRACLE THROUGH TABITHA AND PETER

WEEK 49:
The Disciples Share the Good News

SCRIPTURE REFERENCE: Acts 16:11–15, Mark 16:15
THEME: Sharing the good news of Jesus

The Story: The disciples went to many places to tell others the good news about Jesus, and they met lots of people along the way. In Philippi, they were looking for a place to pray near a river and sat by a group of women. The heart of one woman, Lydia, was opened, and she believed Paul's message. Because of her, all who lived in her house believed and were baptized.

God's Message: The disciples obeyed Jesus when He told them to go into the world and tell people the good news of the Savior. This meant more people heard about Jesus and started to believe in Him. The disciples are not the only ones called to share the good news. All who believe have an important job to do—to share the good news of Jesus with others!

TELL THE GOOD NEWS!

We hear about news—good and bad—every day, but Jesus gives us only good news to share! In the following boxes, make your own newspaper about the good news of Jesus. Each section has a Bible verse to help you with ideas. Write a big title, draw pictures, or write out the verse. Use your creativity and have fun!

Romans 8:39

John 3:16

continued

Tell the Good News! *continued*

John 12:46

Mark 1:4

(See page 169 for answers)

SPREAD GOOD NEWS

Materials:

bag of Skittles
medium or small plate
half cup of warm water

Let's see how sharing the good news of Jesus spreads to others.

Directions: Place the Skittles in a circle on the plate around the edge. The circle should be four or five inches across. Slowly pour the warm water onto the plate just outside the circle of Skittles. Go all the way around the circle. Watch what the colors do!

Lesson: When we tell people about Jesus, the good news spreads, just like the colors from the Skittles. When believers tell the world about Jesus, lives are changed just like the water.

DISCUSS IT!

Why do you think Lydia's whole family believed after she believed?

Have you ever shared the good news about Jesus before? If you had the chance to share the good news today, what would you say?

WEEK 50:
What Will Heaven Be Like?

SCRIPTURE REFERENCE: Matthew 28:16–19, John 14:2–3, Revelation 21:3–27; 22:1–5
THEME: Heaven is waiting for us

The Story: After Jesus rose from the dead, He stayed on Earth for a time. During that time, He appeared to those who doubted that He rose from the grave, and He reminded the disciples to make disciples of all nations. Then Jesus returned to heaven to be with the Father and get heaven ready for us. Heaven will be a place with no tears. Angels will be singing, and there will be no darkness. The city will be made of gold and precious stones. Instead of the sun, God's glory will be the light of heaven forever.

God's Message: Jesus left Earth so He could get our forever home ready. While we wait for that day, Jesus wants us to live our lives for Him and tell others about the amazing place we will live with Jesus forever and ever.

UNSCRAMBLE IT!

Read Revelation 21:3–27 and unscramble the words to complete the sentences. One letter has been included to help.

1. **RETA** God will wipe every `t___`. (Revelation 21:4)

2. **NREOTH** God is seated on a `__r___`. (Revelation 21:5)

3. **WLTEVE** The Holy City has `_w____` gates. (Revelation 21:12)

4. **LDGO** The city is made of pure `_o__`. (Revelation 21:18)

5. **NESTOS** The city foundation is decorated with precious `____e_`. (Revelation 21:19)

6. **TMEPLE** God and the Lamb are the `___p__`. (Revelation 21:22)

7. **GHINT** There will be no `_i___`. (Revelation 21:25)

8. **LFIE** Only the names written in the Lamb's book of `l___` will enter. (Revelation 21:27)

(See page 169 for answers)

WEEK 50: WHAT WILL HEAVEN BE LIKE?

GET YOUR HOUSE READY FOR SPECIAL GUESTS

Materials:

vacuum
broom

duster
cleaning supplies

Let's get your house ready for special guests!

Directions: Vacuum the carpet, sweep the floors, dust the tables, wipe down your kitchen counters, and tidy up your room!

Lesson: What do you and your family do to prepare your home for guests? I'm sure there's some vacuuming, sweeping, and dusting. Heaven will be better than even the cleanest house on Earth. We are going to be special guests in heaven. Jesus is there now getting it ready for us!

DISCUSS IT!

What do you think it will be like in heaven? Will there be sadness or anything bad?

_____

_____

What do we need to do to be with Jesus in heaven?

_____

_____

WEEK 51:
Put on the Armor of God

SCRIPTURE REFERENCE: Ephesians 6:10–20
THEME: Be ready for spiritual battle

The Story: We wear the Armor of God so we can stand against the enemy, the devil. Our battle is not against people or countries; it is a spiritual battle. We don't need to worry. God has given us everything we need to defeat the devil through the Word of God: the Belt of Truth to keep us grounded, the Breastplate of Righteousness to protect our hearts, feet fitted with the Shoes of the Gospel of Peace so we are ready to share the Word of God, the Shield of Faith to block negativity and lies, the Helmet of Salvation to protect our minds, and the Sword of the Spirit to protect us from the devil. This is the Armor of God.

God's Message: We are to put on the full Armor of God to be able to fight in this spiritual battle. This kind of battle doesn't look like the kind we see in the world. This is a battle that happens in our hearts and minds. For example, it is a battle when we struggle to obey our parents, or struggle to be kind when it's hard. When we are filled with God's truth, righteousness, peace, faith, salvation, and Spirit, the devil has no power and no hope of victory! We will win the battle when we wear the Armor of God.

THE ARMOR OF GOD

Write Ephesians 6:11 in the box below. Then fill in the blanks to put together the full Armor of God.

1. The _____ of Truth

2. The _____ of Righteousness

3. The _____ of the Gospel of Peace

4. The _____ of Faith

5. The _____ of Salvation

6. The _____ of the Spirit

WORD BANK

| Belt | Shoes | Helmet |
| Breastplate | Shield | Sword |

(See page 169 for answers)

158   BIBLE STUDY WORKBOOK FOR KIDS

PUT ON THAT ARMOR!

Materials:

big, long roll of paper
markers
a helper

Let's put on the Armor of God!

Directions: Roll out the paper so it is long enough for you to lie flat on. Have your helper trace the outline of your body. Now draw the Armor of God on the traced body and label each piece. Can you remember the names of all the pieces?

Lesson: The person and armor drawn on that paper represent your spiritual body wearing the Armor of God. Hang the paper up in your room to remind you to put on your armor every day!

DISCUSS IT!

Why is spiritual armor important? What are we fighting?

Is there a reason for us to be afraid? How does God help us?

WEEK 52:
Faith that Saves

SCRIPTURE REFERENCE: Luke 7:36–50
THEME: Faith is trusting God

The Story: Jesus was having dinner at a Pharisee's house when a sinful woman showed up because she heard Jesus was there. Her faith and trust in Jesus were so great, she began to cry. She cried so much her tears wet His feet. She used her hair to dry Jesus's feet and poured expensive perfume on them. The Pharisees thought Jesus should not allow her to touch Him because she was such a sinful woman, but Jesus said that her faith in Him had saved her!

God's Message: Faith is trusting in things we cannot see. We cannot see God, but through faith we believe. The Bible tells us stories of many men and women who had faith. They trusted God through the impossible. Through their stories, we see over and over that God is faithful. It is through faith that we trust God will do what He has promised, and it is faith that saves us.

TEST YOURSELF

Read Hebrews 11:4–31 to learn about people who lived by faith. Then test yourself and match each question with its answer. You can check the verses if you get stuck.

1. _____ brought God a better offering than Cain. (Hebrews 11:4)

2. _____ did not die but was taken up by God. (Hebrews 11:5)

3. _____ built an ark. (Hebrews 11:7)

4. _____ gave birth to a son at a very old age. (Hebrews 11:11)

5. _____ was willing to offer Isaac as a sacrifice. (Hebrews 11:17)

6. _____ blessed Jacob and Esau. (Hebrews 11:20)

7. _____ led the Israelites out of Egypt. (Hebrews 11:24–27)

8. _____ welcomed spies and was not killed. (Hebrews 11:31)

    a. Isaac
    b. Sarah
    c. Noah
    d. Abel
    e. Abraham
    f. Moses
    g. Enoch
    h. Rahab

What does Hebrews 11:1 say? Write it below:

_____

(See page 169 for answers)

WEEK 52: FAITH THAT SAVES

TRUST FALL

Material:

an adult partner

Let's practice trusting in something you can't see!

Directions: Stand with your back to the adult. Here's where it gets risky: fall backward! How did you feel right before you fell? How did you feel after?

Lesson: You couldn't see the adult behind you, but you trusted they would not let you crash to the ground. When we trust someone, we have faith in them. It is the same with God. We trust Him, have a relationship with Him, and have faith that He will always care for us!

DISCUSS IT!

What does it mean to have faith? What makes it hard to have faith?

_____

_____

How do you show your faith in Jesus?

_____

_____

ANSWER KEY

WEEK 1 (PAGE 2)

1. light
2. fifth
3. waters
4. plants
5. seas
6. fourth
7. image
8. rested

WEEK 2 (PAGE 5)

1. A
2. B
3. B
4. C
5. A
6. A

WEEK 3 (PAGE 8)

Answers may vary.

WEEK 4 (PAGE 11)

1. D
2. C
3. G
4. H
5. F
6. B
7. E
8. A

WEEK 5 (PAGE 15)

Answers may vary.

Job's qualities: Blameless, had strong morals, feared God, stayed away from evil

What Job lost: donkeys, oxen, farmhands, sheep, shepherds, camels, servants, all his children

How Job reacted: He tore his robe, shaved his head, fell to the ground, and worshipped the Lord.

WEEK 6 (PAGE 18)

Answers may vary.

WEEK 7 (PAGE 21)

1. Isaac's father's name: Abraham
2. Abraham sent the servant to find this for Isaac: a wife
3. The number of camels the servant took with him: 10
4. Where the servant met Rebekah: a well
5. The servant prayed Rebekah would give water to him, and these also: his camels
6. Jewelry that the servant gave Rebekah: gold bracelets
7. Rebekah's brother's name: Laban
8. Isaac's age when he married Rebekah: 40

What were the names of Isaac and Rebekah's two sons? Esau and Jacob

163

WEEK 8 (PAGE 24)

Possible answers:

Esau

  hairy body

  hunter

  liked the outdoors

  sold his birthright

  Isaac's favorite

  held a grudge against Jacob

  wanted to kill Jacob

Jacob

  held on to Esau's heel

  liked staying home

  sold stew for brother's birthright

  Rebekah's favorite

  tricked his father

  got Isaac's blessing

  left home because of Esau's anger

WEEK 9 (PAGE 27)

1. Joseph's brothers were **jealous** that he got a special coat from his father.
2. **Forgiveness** is what God wants us to have in our hearts.
3. Joseph showed his brothers **mercy** when they came to him in Egypt.
4. **Pharaoh** had a dream that Joseph helped him understand.
5. Joseph was made second-in-command in Egypt because he was **wise**.
6. Joseph saved Egypt from **a famine**.
7. Joseph's forgiveness for his brothers caused him to **prosper**.

WEEK 10 (PAGE 31)

1. boy
2. basket
3. daughter
4. bush
5. plagues
6. Israelites
7. Red
8. sea

WEEK 11 (PAGE 34)

Answers may vary.

WEEK 12 (PAGE 37)

Answers may vary.

If you love me, obey my commandments.

WEEK 13 (PAGE 41)

1. Palm
2. Israel
3. prophet
4. Barak
5. Jael
6. Sisera
7. Canaan
8. Lord

WEEK 14 (PAGE 44)

1. C
2. E
3. I
4. J
5. A
6. B
7. H
8. D
9. F
10. G

WEEK 15 (PAGE 47)

1. a famine
2. Ruth and Orpah
3. Ruth
4. Bethlehem
5. Mara
6. leftover grain
7. Boaz

WEEK 16 (PAGE 50)

1. b
2. c
3. c
4. b
5. Jesus, or God's son.

WEEK 17 (PAGE 53)

David

b. Israelite shepherd boy
c. youngest of the family
e. wore no armor
f. played the lyre
i. carried five stones and a sling
j. trusted God's power

Goliath

a. Philistine soldier
d. a giant
g. wore a bronze helmet and armor
h. carried a javelin, sword, and spear
k. relied on his own power

WEEK 18 (PAGE 57)

Answers may vary.

Circle the numbers of things that describe David: 1, 2, 4

WEEK 19 (PAGE 60)

Answers may vary.

WEEK 20 (PAGE 63)

1. C
2. B
3. C
4. B

If you seek God, you will find him.

WEEK 21 (PAGE 66)

Answers may vary.

WEEK 22 (PAGE 69)

| Exodus 3:1–4 | Moses | saw a burning bush |
| Daniel 2:19 | Daniel | a mystery was revealed in a vision |

Ezekiel 1:4	Ezekiel	saw a windstorm in a vision
Isaiah 6:8	Isaiah	said, "Send me!"
Genesis 18:2	Abraham	saw three men (angels) standing nearby
1 Samuel 3:4–5	Samuel	said, "Here I am."
Judges 4:9	Deborah	said, "I will go with you."
Numbers 12:10	Miriam	skin turned white
Jonah 1:3	Jonah	ran from the Lord
Micah 5:2	Micah	foretold Jesus would be born in Bethlehem

WEEK 23 (PAGE 72)

1. C
2. B
3. A
4. B
5. C
6. B

WEEK 24 (PAGE 75)

Answers may vary.

WEEK 25 (PAGE 78)

1. He held a banquet, made a holiday, and gave gifts.
2. She was Jewish.
3. All the Jews in Persia.
4. "Perhaps you were made queen for just such a time as this."
5. She fasted and prayed for three days.
6. "Save/spare my life and the lives of the Jewish people."

WEEK 26 (PAGE 81)

Answers may vary.

WEEK 27 (PAGE 84)

1. Good Shepherd
2. Lamb of God
3. Messiah
4. Immanuel
5. Savior
6. Rabbi
7. Light of the World
8. Redeemer
9. Son of Man

WEEK 28 (PAGE 87)

1. Luke 1:5 Elizabeth was Zechariah's wife.
2. Luke 1:13 "You are to call him John."
3. Luke 1:20 Zechariah could not speak because he didn't believe.
4. Luke 1:26 God sends the angel Gabriel to Nazareth.
5. Luke 1:39–40 Mary hurried to see Elizabeth.
6. Luke 1:41 The baby leaped in Elizabeth's womb.
7. Luke 1:48 The generations will call Mary blessed.
8. Luke 1:56 Mary stayed with Elizabeth for three months.
9. Luke 2:10 "I bring you good news!"

WEEK 29 (PAGE 90)

1. Bethlehem
2. They needed to be counted in the census.

3. Herod
4. Jesus
5. To take Mary as his wife
6. They told others Jesus was born.

WEEK 30 (PAGE 93)

Answers may vary.

Baptism: a ceremony with water that is a sign of faith in God

Messiah: a name for Jesus, meaning "the chosen one"

Repent: to be sorry for a sin and turn away from it

Prophecy: a statement about something that will happen in the future

WEEK 31 (PAGE 96)

Answers may vary.

WEEK 32 (PAGE 99)

1. J - Simon Peter
2. C - Andrew
3. D - James
4. E - Philip
5. I - Nathanael
6. A - Matthew
7. F - Thomas
8. D - John
9. K - James, son of Alphaeus
10. G - Simon the Zealot
11. B - Judas Iscariot
12. H - Judas/Jude/Thaddeus

WEEK 33 (PAGE 102)

1. B
2. A
3. A
4. A
5. C

WEEK 34 (PAGE 105)

Answers may vary.

WEEK 35 (PAGE 108)

1. Nicodemus
2. night
3. miracles
4. born
5. baby
6. wind

WEEK 36 (PAGE 111)

1. D
2. C
3. A
4. B

WEEK 37 (PAGE 115)

Answers may vary.

WEEK 38 (PAGE 118)

1. True
2. False
3. False
4. True
5. True
6. True
7. True
8. False

WEEK 39 (PAGE 121)

1. prodigal: wasteful, spends too much
2. inheritance: money and property you get when a person dies
3. mercy: kindness from someone with power
4. repent: to be sorry for sins
5. parable: a story that teaches a lesson

WEEK 40 (PAGE 124)

1. Nain
2. dead
3. cry
4. get up
5. praised
6. twelve
7. messenger
8. asleep

WEEK 41 (PAGE 127)

Answers may vary.

WEEK 42 (PAGE 130)

Answers may vary.

Here's what could be written on the leaves:

Zacchaeus was a tax collector.

He was too short to see Jesus.

He climbed a tree to see Jesus.

It was a sycamore-fig tree.

Jesus saw him in the tree.

Jesus called him down.

Jesus stayed at his house.

The people saw Zacchaeus as a bad man.

Jesus saw his heart.

Zacchaeus gave half his things to the poor.

He gave four times the amount of money he stole from people.

Jesus gave salvation to the house of Zacchaeus.

WEEK 43 (PAGE 133)

1. G
2. E
3. H
4. A
5. B
6. F
7. C
8. D

WEEK 44 (PAGE 136)

3
2
4
1

WEEK 45 (PAGE 139)

1. Gethsemane
2. James
3. kiss
4. Yours
5. sleeping
6. sword
7. angel
8. blood
9. Annas

WEEK 46 (PAGE 142)

Answers may vary.

WEEK 47 (PAGE 145)

Answers may vary.

Here's what could be written in the boxes:

He hated Christians.

He went on a journey to Damascus.

He was blinded by a light from heaven.

He asked, "Who are You, Lord?"

He was blind for three days.

God healed his blindness through Ananias.

He was baptized.

He preached God's Word.

He tried to join the disciples.

WEEK 48 (PAGE 148)

1. True
2. False
3. True
4. False
5. False
6. True

WEEK 49 (PAGE 152)

Answers may vary.

WEEK 50 (PAGE 155)

1. tear
2. throne
3. twelve
4. gold
5. stones
6. temple
7. night
8. life

WEEK 51 (PAGE 158)

1. Belt
2. Breastplate
3. Shoes
4. Shield
5. Helmet
6. Sword

WEEK 52 (PAGE 161)

1. D
2. G
3. C
4. B
5. E
6. A
7. F
8. H

ABOUT THE AUTHOR

Jenny Ingram lives a ferry ride from Seattle with her husband of twenty-nine years, Paul. She and Paul have 3 great "kids" all in different stages of young-adulthood. In 2004, Jenny began her blog, *Jenny on the Spot*, as an outlet for her love of storytelling. There she has shared stories of life, faith, parenting, and a variety of creative adventures. Her debut book, *Adulting for Christians*, encourages young adults in faith and offers practical advice as they enter a new season of life. Connect with Jenny at *@jennyonthespot* on Instagram or at JennyOnTheSpot.com.